# KIRSTIE'S CHRISTMAS CRAFTS

# KIRSTIE ALLSOPP

# *KIRSTIE'S CHRISTMAS CRAFTS*

---

*MAKE · CREATE*
*GIVE · EAT*

HODDER &
STOUGHTON

First published in Great Britain in 2013 by Hodder & Stoughton
An Hachette UK company

1

A CIP catalogue record for this title is available from the British Library

Hardback ISBN 978 1 444 7 8075 8
Ebook ISBN 978 1 444 7 8076 5

Photography © RTRP 2013

Illustrations by Kuo Kang Chen

Designed by Clare Skeats and Nicky Barneby
Typeset in Harriet Text
Printed and bound by Butler Tanner & Dennis Ltd

Hodder & Stoughton policy is to use papers that are natural, renewable
and recyclable products and made from wood grown in sustainable
forests. The logging and manufacturing processes are expected to conform
to the environmental regulations of the country of origin.

Hodder & Stoughton Ltd
338 Euston Road
London NW1 3BH

www.hodder.co.uk

This book is dedicated to Foxy, 1997–2013, the best Christmas present
I ever had. And also to the work of Home-Start UK, a remarkable charity,
that helps parents and children during difficult times.

# CONTENTS

———

# INTRODUCTION

What could be better than Christmas plus crafts? It's a killer combination. So when I first started making the Christmas programmes, it was a dream come true. Over the last four years, the shows have received the most incredible response. I've had more pictures sent to me on Twitter of homemade crackers, wreaths and stockings than you can shake a sparkly stick at, so being asked to do a book that brings together all the things we've made and more was like being given the golden ticket for Willy Wonka's factory.

I hope this book inspires you and your family to add some extra festive fizz this Christmas. There are seven chapters and more than fifty practical projects that cover every aspect of festive creating, from decorations and gifts to things to make with the children and, arguably the best thing about Christmas, food glorious food. It is full of hints and tips, and has countless lovely pictures to look at.

I've always been a bit of a planner, and my preparation for Christmas kicks off early in October. For me, getting ahead means less stress in December and more time to actually enjoy the build-up with my family and friends. I'm guessing if you have this book that you're a fan of Christmas and therefore won't mind me saying that getting cracking in October isn't crazy – it's a winning tactic. I also think it works out cheaper because you can plan the gifts you're giving, have time to make a few things (which is obviously why you have this book), instead of throwing money at it because it's 22 December and you don't know where the time has gone. That's my theory, anyway!

# KEY PREPPING DATES

## OCTOBER

- Something to get cracking with straight away is Mandy's Advent calendar on page 37 – that's if you want to get it finished by 1 December.

- Start your Christmas present list. Something else that's really handy is to create a Christmas pictures album on your phone so that any time you buy something, you can take a quick snap of it and store it in the album. At a glance I can scan through everything I've bought. There are some great Christmas list apps out there too.

- Make other lists: an online shopping list, a high street list, and a list of local Christmas fairs and shopping events. There's one Christmas fair near me in Devon that's quite late on, but it's so good that I hold out for it. I bought presents for five key people there last year.

- I send an annual email to the parents of all my godchildren, nieces and nephews to find out what they really want. Whether it's Baby Annabell or Sylvanian Families, Lego Ninjago or Moshi Monsters, the polite reply from parents is usually, 'Oh, anything will do,' but when you're five, that is just not true.

- Definitely book a day off work for a midweek shop at the big toy store *before* the Christmas rush begins and everything sells out.

- Amidst all the Christmas planning, don't forget Halloween. We start getting the costumes ready about ten days before, and do a lot of making ourselves, but for my youngest's first-ever Halloween, I dressed him in some Gap glow-in-the-dark skeleton pyjamas. He had just begun walking at the time and he looked so-o-o cute. Those PJs are the best gift, best costume and best multi-tasking outfit ever.

## NOVEMBER

- It's less than eight weeks to Christmas, but remember to buy sparklers, skewers and plenty of marshmallows for Guy Fawkes Night. It could be perfect timing for a test run making the passion fruit marshmallows on page 149. They're really good.

- This is a good month to start making some of the really Christmassy projects that could transform your home. The stocking on page 20 takes about a day, while the bunting on page 17 could be a rolling project throughout the month, depending on how much you want to make.

- I love the candles on page 87 and they're perfect for dotting around if you're thinking of throwing a drinks party in December.

- Check out the Christmas decorations, especially the fairy lights. There is nothing worse than starting to decorate the tree and discovering all the lights are dud. They sell out unbelievably fast, so waiting until mid-December to discover yours don't work could leave your tree without a twinkle. Disaster!

- If you're cooking with white onions, save the skins for the dip-dyed placemats project on page 93. The results are beautiful.

- The last Sunday in November is traditionally known as Stir-up Sunday, the day to make your Christmas pudding so that the flavours have time to mature. While you're at it, make your mincemeat for the filo mince pies on page 172 and store in a cool, dry place until you're ready to start baking.

### DECEMBER

- If you haven't finished Mandy's Advent calendar by now, perhaps it's time to put it somewhere safe until next year!

- If you're hosting Christmas Day lunch, start planning your menu. There's a delicious rib of beef recipe on page 167, and the ham on page 164 is one of my favourite meals on earth.

- I put up my tree in mid-December, usually twelve days before Christmas. When it comes to other decorations, I

think the kissing balls on page 35 are brilliant things to make with friends at home as a little pre-Christmas party that gets you into the festive spirit.

- I make a point of visiting a few local Christmas food fairs. There's usually a mulled wine seller, and you can wander around sipping and picking up delicious Christmas treats. I always buy cheese for after dinner, and special condiments, but will definitely be making the Boxing Day chutney on page 138.

- Keep a few hours aside on Christmas Eve for preparing some of the food for the big day. It makes such a difference to be ahead of the game, and will help keep the next day's timings on track.

- Oh, and whatever you do, don't forget to cut the tops off the carrots for Father Christmas's reindeers.

# DECK THE HALLS

---

## THE WREATH, TREE AND OTHER DECORATIONS

If aliens landed on my doorstep on Christmas Eve, I'd want them to take one look at my house and know that something big was being celebrated. So if you're looking for less is more, move away now!

What is now Christmas Day, on 25 December, was originally a huge pagan festival. It was popularised as the date for Christmas not because Christ was born on that day, but because it was already celebrated as the birthday of the sun. This ancient festival of light in the darkest days of winter remains a strong and beautiful influence on our Christmas decorations today.

If we were playing a word association game and someone said 'Christmas', I'd say 'Quality Street'. For me these chocolates are the very essence of the festive season. I love the sparkle and glitter; I adore the golds, reds and greens. I try to make my home feel like a box of Quality Street at Christmas, taking inspiration from the colours, and adding lights, glass balls and, most importantly, tinsel. I don't hold with a tinsel-free Christmas. To me a tree with no tinsel is like gin and tonic with no ice or lemon. I've always loved tinsel, and since my recent discovery that a lot of it is actually made in Wales, I am even more devoted. Check out www.festive.co.uk for a video on how they make tinsel. I defy you not to be won over.

There are some decorations I bring out every year, like the heart garland on page 12 and a lovely paper-cut snowflake made for me by photographer Fiona Murray, which I hang in the window. They always make me smile. There are memories or stories attached to all my favourite decorations. Call me sentimental, but I think that's one of the true joys of Christmas.

Now, what do you think of decorating the outside of your house? It's a contentious issue and there is huge snobbery surrounding it. I am a recent convert. I've always loved going to New York in December for the shopping, the lights and the Americans' absolute devotion to the festive season, but it was my trip to the New York suburbs that got me hooked on outdoor decorations. If you ever go, they do bus tours of all the houses lit up like Christmas trees. I had the best time filming at the Pansini family home in Staten Island. The father, Steve, has around 400 animations that he's collected over the last twenty-three years, and it takes him and a bunch of loyal friends twenty-one days to set the whole thing up. It is utterly incredible. Inspired, I bought some lights in the shape of reindeers, snowmen and a Father Christmas, and the kids love them. They've now become an integral part of our festivities and mark the countdown to the big day. I say even if your neighbours are horrified by the big, flashing neon decorations in your front garden, if they make you and the children happy, go for it. If, like Steve and me, you decide on a slice of neon this year, you can buy some cracking outdoor decorations in garden centres and, of course, online.

It fills me with joy to see more and more places in Britain getting into the festive spirit. Come December, the whole village of Eathorpe in Warwickshire is a shrine to outdoor Christmas decorations, and the display rivals anything seen in the New York suburbs. It's worth a visit if you want to capture a little piece of Christmas magic in the UK.

I always have a generous wreath on my front door. Once you've committed to having a wreath, it doesn't make much difference in time or money if you go bigger, and there's far more danger of a wreath looking stingy than over the top. I usually try to make my own, and I always have a lot of fun using gold spray (a Christmas decoration must-have) on pine cones, nuts, cinnamon sticks and all sorts. The beauty of making your own is that you can add whatever you like and it sets the tone for the decorations inside your home. There's a beautiful Christmas wreath you can have a go at making on page 9.

Once inside my house, tinsel winds its way up the stairs, around the handrail and through the banisters. In the past I've also made an evergreen garland for my staircase, which looks incredible. Children, particularly the older, more responsible ones, love to be sent out foraging for pine cones and greenery, but it's best to give them some reference pictures before they head out. My lot come back

with loads, and it never goes to waste: I put holly on top of every picture and along our fireplace and windowsills. What can't be found outside can easily be bought, so if you have the time and budget, an evergreen garland is glorious. But I'm also a tinsel girl and I reckon it works brilliantly too.

In Devon our tree is always in the hall. The ceilings are high, so every year we get a tall tree from the same local grower, Nick Steven in the Blackdown Hills. Nick lets me loose in his field around October to select my tree, and we tie a thick ribbon around the chosen one to reserve it. This saves him having to deal with my fussiness at his busiest time of year. (I did once chop down my own tree in front of a very worried-looking TV director. I can understand why the sight of me and a saw just a few feet away was pretty terrifying.)

Decorating the tree is a job and a half. It takes ladders, lots of little helpers and a whole day to cover it all around from top to bottom. I don't hold back even slightly, and the effort is worth it. Anyone who comes through our front door heads straight for the tree. I put my lights on first and then spend a *long* time covering the wires and plastic with tinsel so that when I switch on the lights, the tinsel reflects their sparkle, giving a beautiful glittering effect. My decorations have been collected over time. I don't necessarily use the same things every Christmas, and I do buy a few new things each year because there are always some that get broken. Last year at my son's school they were selling off a whole

load of blue baubles to raise money and, when no one bought them, I decided to take the lot and go for a blue bauble and green tinsel theme on my tree. It looked fantastic. I used lots and lots of ribbon to cover the thin wire tying the baubles onto the tree. The ribbon is everything. The more there is, the merrier I am.

Second-hand decorations are something I always look out for, and not just at Christmas when they're more desirable and therefore more expensive. You may cringe at the thought, but it's worth keeping an eye out for them all year round. I've spotted many a glass bauble and boxes of vintage decorations at both New York and Paris flea markets in the springtime, and all over the UK, especially at antiques fairs. As no one else tends to be interested, I get them at a good price. It's the same after Christmas. If you can bear it, the sales are great places to pick up bargain lengths of tinsel that you can store and bring out new next year.

Making your own decorations is brilliant, and this chapter is full of ideas. The kissing balls (see page 35) are utterly therapeutic to make, and you can customise them to fit your colour theme perfectly. (Of course, you should always have a colour theme!) Personally, I'm obsessed with paper decorations, and there is a lovely 3D snowflake garland on page 31 that is extraordinarily simple and cheap to make. The effect is amazing, and it looks lovely strung up across a window or between pictures.

However you decide to deck your halls, don't hold back. Christmas is about having fun and letting go. I say embrace it in all its variety.

# CHRISTMAS WREATH

Floral designer Kitten Grayson makes magical Christmas wreaths, thick with festive foliage and flowers that look sensational on any front door. I've made a few wreaths in my time, and you can definitely save money doing your own. The trick is not to scrimp when applying the sack moss to the wire frame as it's the basis for a really sumptuous and full design. You can buy sack moss from your local florist or garden centre, but make sure it's nice and damp as that will help your evergreens to stay fresh and lush. If you want to get straight on to decorating the wreath, skip the first two steps below and buy a ready-made base instead.

## YOU WILL NEED

———

Reel wire • 2 cm raised wire wreath frame • Sack moss (make sure it's nice and moist) • 6–7 big pine branches • Eucalyptus (because it smells divine) • Scissors • Extra foliage, such as myrtle berry, mimosa, holly and ivy • 5–7 stems hypericum berries • 7 stems dried English hydrangeas • Reindeer moss (ours looked feathery and silver) • Glitter (optional) • Gauge wire (thicker than reel wire and comes in pre-cut lengths) • Optional extra decorations, such as white wax flowers, pine cones, dried orange slices, cinnamon sticks and glittered-up berries, black peppercorns, dried roses and crab apples

1  To make the moss base, unravel a bit of your reel wire and attach it with a twist to the frame. Now begin placing generous handfuls of sack moss around the frame, packing it tightly together and winding the reel wire around it tightly as you go. Whatever you do, don't scrimp – the moss should feel thick and dense. Do a second layer of moss to really thicken it out, and continue binding it with the wire. Don't worry about it not being neat; the moss won't be seen when it's dressed.

2  When full, turn the wreath over and cut the wire, leaving a 20 cm end. Push it from back to front through the centre of the moss, then back again. Do this a few times, until the wire is eaten up by the moss, then twist the last bit around the inner ring on the back of the frame.

3  Cut the pine and eucalyptus into pieces about 10–15 cm long and begin grouping them into fan-like clusters. They should look luscious and full with no gaps. Snip off any naked pointy bits.

4  Place the wreath right side up and lay the first fan-cluster of greenery on top of the moss. Secure by wrapping reel wire around the stems. Continue covering the moss with small fan-clusters, securing them tightly with wire, until the front of the wreath is completely covered.

5  To cover the inside of the wreath, add smaller, finger-sized pieces of greenery and secure them with wire. While doing so, take a good look at the shape of your wreath and lightly tie down any stray foliage. You want it to look even all round. When finished, tie off the wire as in step 2.

6  Now to the fun bit – decorating. It's essential to have a theme – ours was hypericum berries, dried hydrangeas and reindeer moss – but dried roses are exquisite, and glittered crab apples look very Christmassy too. Before you start, look at your wreath and think about where you're going to place things. Odd numbers work best, and you must always aim for balance.

7  Cut the stems of your flowers and berries on a slant so they have a pointy end. Pierce the first berry stem deep into the moss, then continue adding the other berry stems at regular intervals around the wreath.

8  Now add the hydrangeas in the same way. If you struggle to get things well into the moss, simply attach them using the gauge wire.

9  To add the reindeer moss, bend a length of wire in half, pierce it through the side of a clump and push the ends through to the back of the wreath. Bend into a loop and twist the ends to fasten. The loop shouldn't be visible with this method. Continue adding reindeer moss around the wreath in this way, filling in the gaps between the hydrangeas and berries.

10  To make a hook, take two long gauge wires and bend them into a hook shape. Locate the top of your wreath and pierce the gauge wire through from the back and around the outer ring of your frame. Bring the hook ends up at the back and secure with a twist.

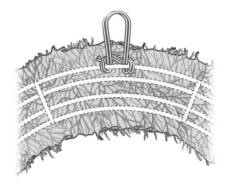

*Pine is great for wreaths because of its bulky and lasting nature. It's also easy to find.*

*Get the children foraging in the garden for branches, twigs, winter berries, holly and ivy. What you need are things that flex and bend, and that will add texture to the wreath.*

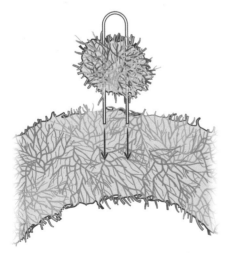

# HEART GARLAND

This garland has to be one of my all-time favourite Christmas decorations – the type of thing you bring out year after year because it perfectly captures the sentiment of the season. It's so simple to do, yet utterly satisfying.

Before you start making your garland, get out your pinking shears. If you don't have any, buy some. They're not cheap, but they're worth every penny if you're a fan of textile and sewing crafts, and they'll come in handy throughout this book. Pinking shears are normally used to minimise fraying, but with the Bondaweb already doing that job, I like to use them for decorative effect. Once you've got that sorted, it's all about the fabrics. I'm always harping on about keeping a ragbag of bits that you might eventually find a use for, and here you can. You can make your hearts from any old scraps or memorable pieces you've saved, or even from new bits you've wanted to buy. Remember, you'll need to measure the place where you want to hang the garland before you buy the cord, and double the length to allow for all the knots and a graceful curve.

## *YOU WILL NEED*

Pencil, tracing paper and card • Scissors • Selection of fabrics • Bondaweb (iron-on fabric adhesive) • Pins • Bright embroidery thread • Sewing needle • Pinking shears • Polyester stuffing • Gold mini bells (available from craft shops) • Fine craft wire • Cord, twice the length of the space where the garland will hang • Glue

1 Trace around the heart shape on page 226, then transfer it to a piece of cardboard. Cut around the heart outline to create a template. (If you have one, a heart-shaped biscuit cutter can be used instead.)

2 Take a piece of fabric, cut a piece of Bondaweb to the same size and place it, paper side up, on the wrong side of the fabric. Press with a hot iron.

3 Place the heart template on the paper, trace around it as many times as you want, then cut out the shapes.

4 Peel off the Bondaweb and place two hearts together, right side out. Pin them together about 1 cm from the edge, leaving a 2.5 cm gap above one side of the point to insert the stuffing later. Starting above the gap, hand-sew along the line of pins with a basic running stitch using a bright embroidery thread. Don't sew over the gap.

5  Using a hot iron, press carefully but firmly around the edge of the heart outside the stitching to glue the fabric together.

6  Now for my favourite bit. Using pinking shears, trim around the edges of the heart to create a decorative zigzag effect.

7  Take some of the filling and stuff the heart, taking care not to overfill it. What you want is a softly padded heart, not a hard unyielding one. Sew up the gap with the same running stitch as before to finish it off neatly.

8  Sew a bell onto the top of the heart, then take a piece of wire about 7.5 cm long and pierce it through the heart on either side of the bell. Twist the ends together to form a loop. Continue making hearts in the same way until you have enough for your length of garland.

9  To add more glitter and jingle, thread little bunches of golden bells onto shorter pieces of wire, then twist the ends together to form a loop for hanging.

10  Take your piece of cord, tie a loop in one end and apply glue to the other to prevent it fraying in the next step. Set aside to dry.

11  Using the glued end of the cord, thread it through the loop of a heart and tie a knot to hold it in place. Now add a bunch of bells in the same way. Continue adding hearts and bells, arranging them alternately at regular intervals a few centimetres apart, and knotting the cord so they don't slide around.

12  When everything has been attached, tie a loop in the glued end of the cord and hang it up.

*Keep all scraps of fabric from sewing projects, old curtains and dresses for small craft ideas like this garland.*

# FESTIVE BUNTING

What is it about strings of triangles that makes people so happy? I reckon it's because nothing says 'celebration' quite like bunting. I know it's traditionally a summer thing, but it really works in December too. This Christmas you can make your very own swathes of festive-themed triangles courtesy of Georgie Kirby at The Big Beautiful Bunting Company. When Georgie first started making bunting for big events, she tested its durability by sending her fisherman husband out to sea dressed in her colourful flags, so trust me, this bunting is made to last. Follow this pattern and it will become an heirloom you can pass on to your children.

You will need a sewing machine for ease and speed, but a rotary cutter, which also speeds things up, is optional. All the templates you need – the basic triangle plus the gold appliqués – are on pages 223–4. This project is for 2 metres of bunting, but you can make as much as you like.

## *YOU WILL NEED*

———

Scissors • 1 metre tartan fabric • Pencil, tracing paper and card • Tailor's chalk • 1 metre plain red or green fabric • 50 cm gold fabric • Pins • Sewing machine • Matching or contrasting machine threads • Crochet hook or knitting needle • Cotton tea towel (optional) • 3 metres velvet ribbon, 2.5 cm wide • Tape measure

1  Cut your tartan fabric into two large rectangles measuring 40 × 100 cm. Lay one on top of the other, right sides together.

2  Trace around template A on page 222, then transfer it to a piece of card. Cut around it to create a template. Place the template on the tartan fabric and trace around it three times with tailor's chalk. Cut around the outlines so you have six triangles in total. Repeat this process with the plain fabric.

3  Trace around templates B, C and D on pages 223–4, then transfer to card and cut them out. Place the templates on the gold fabric and trace around them with tailor's chalk: you will need one circle, one rectangle and two small triangles. Cut the circle in half and cut the rectangle into six long strips.

4 Lay out three of the plain fabric triangles, arrange the gold shapes and strips over them and then pin in place. Trim the strips to length, then set the excess aside with the remaining gold shapes to decorate another length of bunting if you wish.

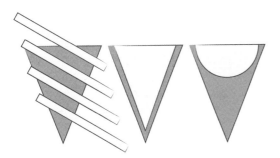

5 Thread your sewing machine with either a matching gold thread or a contrasting red or green thread. Sew the gold shapes onto the plain fabric triangles using a medium zigzag stitch around the edge.

6 Lay the last plain triangles over the decorated triangles, right sides together, and pin just the long sides together about 1 cm from the edge. Sew along them with a simple straight stitch.

7 Turn the pendants right side out, pushing a crochet hook or knitting needle into the point of each one to give it a sharp, professional finish.

8 Steam-iron the pendants, but cover the gold fabric (if synthetic) with a cotton tea towel to prevent it from melting. Trim the open edge of your decorated pendants neatly and set aside.

9 Pin, stitch and turn the tartan triangles as in steps 6 and 7, then steam-iron and trim them as in step 8. Arrange all the pendants in the order you wish them to hang and stack them in a pile.

10 Fold the ribbon in half lengthways and iron along the crease through a damp cloth. Re-thread your sewing machine with a colour that matches or contrasts with the ribbon.

11 Measure 40 cm along the folded ribbon, then tuck your first pendant inside and pin all four layers together. Leave a 2 cm gap and pin your next pendant in the same way. Repeat until all six pendants are pinned in place. Machine along the ribbon, making sure you stitch through all the layers, and continue for 40 cm beyond the last pendant. Trim off any excess and hang your lovely bunting.

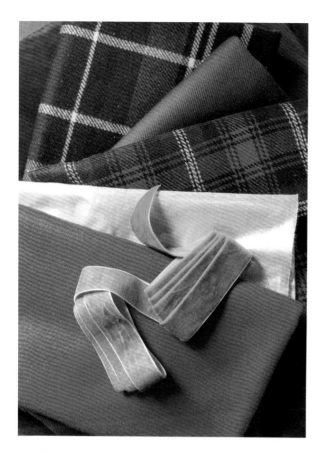

Wool-based fabrics need a softer tension than cotton fabrics, so adjust the tension dial on your machine and practise on scraps of each fabric before you sew. It's also a good idea to practise sewing through several layers because the thickness can also affect the tension required.

A lovely way to display bunting is to hang it from the arms of a central chandelier and stretch it out to each corner of the room, as we did last summer at the vintage wedding of our friends, Amy and Craig.

To clean the bunting, simply sponge with warm water and dry naturally.

# OVERSIZED CHRISTMAS STOCKING

I love this oversized Christmas stocking by designer Alice Begg. It's 62cm long, with a 30 cm opening and a 47 cm foot, a beautiful thing to behold and very, very Christmassy. Its only downside is that filling it could break the bank! My advice? Just tell everyone that the beauty of this giant sock is digging all the way down to the big toe to find the treasure.

The tradition of hanging stockings near the fireplace on Christmas Eve stems from the story of St Nicholas, who took gifts and happiness to those in need. When he came upon an impoverished widower who couldn't afford a dowry for any of his three daughters, he dropped three bags of gold coins down the chimney and they landed in the girls' stockings drying by the fire. That's why oranges, representing the gold bags, and foil-wrapped chocolate coins are traditionally put in Christmas stockings to this day.

Alice made our striped stocking using an old linen sack, a piece of red velvet and pretty cream lace. All these things came from the Cloth Shop on Portobello Road in London, one of my favourite shops. If you have a fabric stash at home, rummage through and see if any of it will come in useful for this project. If not, look online or in markets and shops for offcuts or second-hand pieces in colours and styles you like.

## YOU WILL NEED

6 sheets of A4 paper · Sellotape · Pencil · Scissors · Fabric, such as tweed, a bright wool or canvas stripe, for the stocking · Pins · Sewing machine and suitable thread · Contrasting fabric, such as velvet, for binding · Tailor's chalk · Tape measure · Pretty trim, such as brocade, ribbon, lace or fringing · Hand sewing needle

1 Arrange the A4 sheets in a large rectangle and tape them together. Draw a stocking outline on the rectangle following the scale diagram on page 000. You can, of course, make it any size you like, but remember to keep the opening nice and wide so you can fit in lots of presents. Cut around the outline.

2 Place your stocking fabric piece(s) right sides together. Pin the template on to the fabric, then cut around it.

3 Remove the template, then pin the stocking pieces together about 1 cm from the edge, leaving the top open. Machine the stocking, along the line of pins, then turn it right side out.

4   To make the binding for the opening, open out your contrasting fabric and use tailor's chalk to mark out a strip 2 cm longer than the opening and whatever width you like. Ours was 62 cm long and 24 cm wide, as I like quite a thick band at the top. If you're working with small pieces of fabric, stitch them together to get the length and width you want.

5   Fold and pin a single hem on one long edge of the binding, then machine neatly. Fold the binding in half widthways, right sides together. Pin the two raw ends together, then machine about 1 cm from the edges.

6   Place the raw edge of the binding around the opening of the stocking, right sides together and about 4 cm below it, and sew it in place.

7   Fold the neatened edge of the binding inside the stocking and pin it along the line of stitching you've just sewn. Machine very close to the pinned edge all the way around, or sew by hand

if you prefer. The finished binding should stand higher than the actual stocking

8   To make a loop for hanging the stocking, cut a strip of the binding fabric about 20 cm long and 5 cm wide. Fold in half lengthways, right sides out, then tuck in the raw edges and pin together. Machine close to the pinned edge, then hand-sew the loop to the lower edge of the binding.

9   Pin your trim to the seam where the binding meets the stocking, making sure it covers where you have sewn on the loop. Hand-sew in place

*The stocking can be as simple or as embellished as you like. For a fancy finish, stitch pompoms, hearts or bells around the border.*

# NEEDLEFELT ROBIN

There are several ways of needlefelting; each gives brilliant results, but this one is my personal favourite because it's so easy. You'll need a special needlefelting mat that resembles an upturned brush, plus a spring-loaded punch that contains sharp, barbed needles, and then you're off.

Jayne Emerson showed me how to make this lovely Christmas robin decoration. You simply place fleece over the felt design and stamp the punch up and down to entangle the fibres.

I put my robin on a stick, but you could create a hanging hook instead by pleating some fibres and stamping them in place at the top of the bird's body.

## *YOU WILL NEED*

---

Tailor's chalk pencil · Sheet of brown felt · Scissors · Scrap of black felt · Clover mat and tool · Woollen fleece in brown, red, white and grey · Feather · Needle and thread · 2 beads, for eyes · Long skewer · Brown florist's tape · Glue (optional)

1 Using the tailor's chalk, draw two bird shapes and two wings, as seen on page 27, onto the brown felt. Cut out the shapes.

2 Cut a small triangular shape for the beak from the scrap of black felt and set aside.

3 Put one of the body shapes on the Clover mat. Take a small tuft of brown fleece and lay it on the felt, then begin lightly punching the Clover tool up and down (watch your fingers as the needles are very sharp). It doesn't matter if your fleece spills over the edges: if you stamp lightly, you can easily rectify mistakes, and you can also trim the bird later. Keep lifting the robin up to avoid needlefelting it to the mat. Continue adding fleece to the bird in the appropriate colours and places (see opposite) – rather like painting with fleece.

8 Stuff the robin lightly with a small amount of brown fleece, add the tail feather, then seal the gap with the Clover tool. (You might want to trim your feather into proportion with your robin, but I rather like the unrealistic flamboyance of mine.)

9 Stitch two beads onto the face for the eyes.

10 Wrap the skewer in the florist's tape. Make a small hole on the underside of the bird by delicately pulling the two sides apart, and insert the sharp end of the skewer. Add a little glue if necessary, or take a single needle from the Clover tool and use to felt the skewer in place.

4 Once you are happy with your design, repeat it on the other bird shape (just remember the two sides should be facing opposite directions so that they match up when put together).

5 Repeat the needlefelting process with the robin's two wings.

6 Now needlefelt a wing to each robin shape; you will only need to punch at the base of the wing to create a 3D effect.

7 Place the two sides of the bird together, insert the beak and punch around the edges to secure. You will need to hold the wings out of the way, and you should also leave a small gap under the bird towards the tail end.

# FELT HEART

This little felt heart is something I learnt to make in Lapland a few Christmases ago. It's simple and sweet, and looks so pretty hanging on a tree or door, or over coat hooks or cupboard handles. You can make a fair few in just a couple of hours. Choose different colours and ribbons to match your Christmas colour theme.

## *YOU WILL NEED*

---

Pencil • Paper • Scissors • Pins • Red felt fabric • 1 × 50 cm length of 4 mm ribbon • Needle • Thread, either matching or contrasting • Polyester stuffing or sheep fleece • 2 small beads • 2 small buttons

1  Draw a heart shape on paper and cut it out. Pin it to the felt and cut out two hearts.

2  Take the piece of ribbon and fold it in half. Place it down the centre of one heart so the loop sticks out at the top and the ends hang down below. Place the other heart on top and pin both together.

3  Using a running stitch, sew around the heart about 5 mm from the edge, but leave a 2.5 cm opening for stuffing.

4  Stuff the heart with fleece through the opening, then stitch closed.

5  Thread one or two beads onto the ribbon at the bottom of the heart, tying a knot to keep them in place.

6  Sew a contrasting button on both sides of the heart for decoration.

# 3D SNOWFLAKE GARLAND

I love, love, love paper decorations for every occasion, and I always have them in my house at Christmas. That said, they're pretty pricey to buy, so learning how to make your own is a real saving.

The great thing about paper is that it's versatile and nowhere near as scary as working with more expensive materials. If you go wrong, you just start again with relatively little cost and fuss.

This project by super-talented paper artist Clare Pentlow is a lovely 3D paper snowflake. You can hang clusters of them from the ceiling or create a garland for a wall or window by attaching them to a length of ribbon or string.

A great piece of advice from Clare is to make a trial snowflake with cheap wrapping paper. Once you've mastered the technique, you can start to experiment with different colours and textures of paper, such as metallic or glittery sheets.

## *YOU WILL NEED*

Paper (wrapping paper is ideal) · Scissors · Glue stick · Hole punch · Ribbon

1 Fold a square piece of paper diagonally into quarters. (We used a 7 × 7 cm square.)

2 Starting a few millimetres from the two double folds, cut 3–4 lines parallel to the four open edges and cut right through the thickest fold. Try to space the cuts as evenly as possible. Ours were 5–10 mm apart. When you open out the triangle it should look like this:

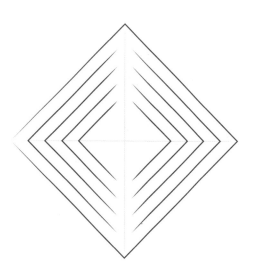

3 Roll the central triangles into one another and glue together, as shown below.

4 Turn the paper over and join the next pair of triangles as shown below.

5 Repeat this process, turning the paper over for each pair of triangles, and you should

eventually end up with a 3D diamond shape as shown below, on the left. Repeat steps 1–5 to make another five diamonds.

6 Join three of the diamonds at one end to make the shape below. Repeat with the remaining three diamonds, then join all six together in the centre. Finally, join the sides of the diamonds.

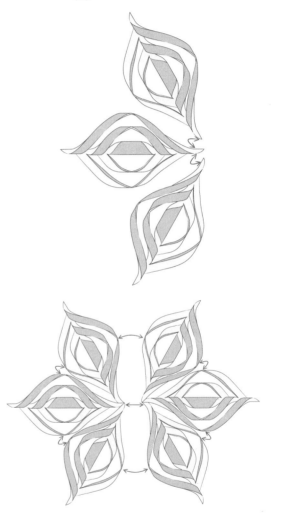

7 Punch a hole in one of the snowflake points, thread ribbon through it and hang up.

*Try varying the spacing of the cuts you make to create different patterns.*

*Cut decorative edges using pinking shears, or snip other shaped edges with small scissors.*

*Try using paper with different colours on either side to make the triangles in step 4 easier to identify.*

*Make snowflake bunting by threading your cut-outs onto a long ribbon and knotting them in position.*

# KISSING BALLS

Dating from medieval times, the original kissing ball was a rough arrangement of Christmas greenery with a plaster figure of the baby Jesus in the middle. It was hung from the ceiling and said to impart love and blessings to those who passed underneath. By Victorian times it had evolved into something quite different. A potato or an apple was used as a base, and sprigs of evergreens and sweet herbs were stuck into it until it positively bristled with them. The resulting 'sweet ball' not only looked beautiful, it smelled good too, which no doubt was a real bonus in the days before daily showers and deodorant. The choice of herbs, flowers and greenery was significant, as each had a symbolic meaning, but by the end of the nineteenth century, the kissing ball unequivocally represented love and romance.

These days the most popular types are mistletoe kissing balls at Christmas, and floral kissing balls for bridal arrangements. Modern versions of the kissing ball can be made with all sorts of materials, ranging from flowers and evergreens to paper, plastic, sequins and beads.

Interior designer Sue Timney's interpretation of the tradition is definitely one of my favourites. This is a brilliant pre-Christmas craft to do with a group of friends. You don't need a tremendous amount of skill or concentration, just enough chairs and a table to spread all your materials on, plus a couple of bottles of wine. Simply make as many decorated balls as you can until the wine's finished.

## *YOU WILL NEED*

Saucer, about 18 cm in diameter · Selection of coloured tissue paper · Pencil · Scissors · PVA glue and small paintbrush · Polystyrene ball (any size you like, but ours was 10 cm) · Selection of buttons, sequins, beads, jewels, feathers or whatever you wish · Pearl-headed pins · Loose-cover pins (these are like croquet hoops with two pointed ends) · Tartan ribbon

1 Place the saucer upside down on a sheet of tissue paper and draw around it twice: you need two circles for each ball. Cut out the circles.

2 Paint the lower half of the ball with a thin layer of glue. Stick the first tissue circle to it, working from the bottom towards the centre and smoothing it with your hands. Repeat this process with the other half of the ball. Set aside to dry for 1½ hours. If you want to speed things along, you can use a hairdryer, but do make sure the ball is dry before moving on to step 3.

3  Now it's time to decorate the ball. I used buttons in various colours and mother-of-pearl and attached them to the ball by pushing a pearl-headed pin through them and into the polystyrene. Large buttons might need two pins to hold them in place, and a four-holed button might look best with four pins in it. Do what pleases you and keep going until the whole ball is covered with brightly covered decorations.

4  Take one or two loose-cover pins, depending on the weight of your ball, and insert in the top of the ball. This is the point from which the ball will be hung, so to give extra support you might like to apply some glue to the prongs of the pin before sticking it in. If so, allow it to dry before the next step.

5  Decide where you want to hang your ball and cut a double length of tartan ribbon to the appropriate depth. Thread it through the pin(s) at the top of the ball and knot the ends together. Hang it on your tree. Perfect!

*It's a good idea to pin the large buttons first, distributing them evenly, then use the smaller buttons to fill the gaps.*

*You can pick up beautiful buttons from charity shops, antiques markets or online. I've come across boxes of vintage buttons for as little as £4, and individual buttons for just a few pennies.*

*If your decorations (e.g. feathers) will completely cover the ball, you can skip the papering step and apply your chosen decorative bits directly to the glue. Before you start, though, do wrap a strip of sticky tape around the 'waist' of the ball. Once the decorations are dry, peel off the tape, wrap a length of tartan ribbon around the ball and secure with pearl-headed pins. Hang as in steps 4 and 5.*

# QUILTED ADVENT CALENDAR

The creative crafter Mandy Shaw is a true Christmas spirit. She once made this incredible quilted advent calendar as a gift for me and my family. When deciding which Christmas crafts I wanted to put in this book, Mandy's calendar was a must. A word of warning, though: it might take you until next Christmas to finish it, especially if you've never attempted a sewing project on this scale before. However, I think the end result is absolutely worth the time and effort it requires. My calendar is now a treasured heirloom and I hope yours will be just as special to your family too.

The finished size is roughly 86 × 112 cm, and the wonderful thing is that it makes use of old scraps of fabric, which are sewn using a quick strip patchwork method. While this isn't difficult, it does require accurate cutting, so patience and somewhere quiet are needed. A useful tip is to lightly spray-starch all your fabric because this will make the folding nice and sharp. Also, using a 1 cm or ¼ inch seam foot on your sewing machine will help to make your seams accurate. Just take your time following Mandy's instructions and it will all come together beautifully.

## *YOU WILL NEED*

Rotary cutter, ruler and mat **or** tape measure, ruler and scissors ·
20 × 105 cm plain fabric, for headboard · 105 × 115 cm soft calico, for sheet ·
8 different fabrics, each 10 × 36 cm, for quilt cover · 50 × 107 cm plain red
fabric, for central block and sashing · Sewing machine and suitable
thread · Tacking thread and sewing needle

### FOR THE TREE AND SASHING
Tracing paper and pencil · 30 cm Bondaweb (iron-on webbing) ·
15 × 15 cm green fabric, for tree · Contrasting embroidery thread and sewing
needle · Red/white checked fabric, for bucket (and bunting if you
wish) · Yellow felt, for star on tree · Pins

### FOR THE BORDER, LAYERING AND QUILTING
46 × 107 cm patterned fabric, for border · 102 × 152 cm backing fabric ·
102 × 152 cm cotton wadding · Masking tape · Safety pins or spray fabric
adhesive · Quilting threads and crewel embroidery needles

FOR THE EMBELLISHMENTS

3.4 metres wide ricrac (optional) · 12 large red buttons and various small
ones · Buttons numbered 1–25 · String of miniature Christmas lights ·
50 cm narrow ricrac, for bunting (optional)

FOR THE BINDING

25 × 107 cm red fabric

FOR THE FACES AND HAIR

8 cm squares of different coloured calico, for faces · Scraps of thick wadding,
for stuffing faces · Pigma permanent pens, for faces · Blusher · Wool,
cotton, raffia, string, mohair or unspun fleece in various colours, for
hair · Glue · Embroidery threads (optional) · Narrow ribbons · Beads

FOR THE HANGING

88 × 13 cm fabric, for sleeve · 90 cm pole · Ribbon or string · Drawing pins
(optional) · Treats, such as crayons, pencil sharpeners, rubbers, notelets,
small toys, lottery tickets, tissues, mini toiletries, hairslides, lip balm, etc.

---

A 6mm seam allowance has been added to
all measurements.

The numbered buttons, miniature lights
and marker pens are all available from
www.dandeliondesigns.co.uk.

1  Start by cutting the fabrics, as follows:
**Headboard:** cut one piece 4 × 36 cm
**Sheet:** cut one piece 28 × 36 cm
**Quilt cover:** cut one piece 9 × 36 cm
**Central block:** cut one piece 15 × 19 cm

BEDS

2  Machine the bed strips together widthways
in the correct order, i.e. headboard, sheet,
quilt cover. Press the seams open.

3  Cut the sewn fabric into three strips 12 cm
wide. There will be some wastage, which is
security in case a cut strip goes wonky.

4  Fold the sheeting so it forms a 2.5 cm
border at the top of the quilt and press the
edge. Align the sheet with the bottom of the
quilt at the back, fold and press, then bring
the remainder of the sheeting back up above

the border to form the bottom sheet. Repeat
with the remaining strips to make two more
beds. Repeat steps 1–4 to make another
twenty-one beds (twenty-four in all).

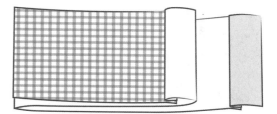

5  Make sure all the beds measure 12 × 17 cm,
then tack down both sides of each one to keep
the layers in place.

TREE

6  Trace the tree, bucket and star templates on
page 228. Transfer them to the Bondaweb and
cut them out roughly. Place the Bondaweb tree
on the wrong side of the green tree fabric and
iron to fuse them together. Cut the shape out
neatly, peel off the backing paper and iron the
tree to the red central block. Using a

contrasting embroidery thread, blanket stitch around the outside of the tree. Repeat this process for the bucket and star.

### SASHING

7  The strips that are stitched around the squares are called sashing. Cut the remaining sashing fabric into strips 5 cm wide, and from these cut the following lengths: 2 × 94 cm, 6 × 69 cm, and 18 × 17 cm.

8  Lay out the beds on the table, five across and five down with the tree in the middle, and juggle them around until you like the arrangement.

9  Insert the 17 cm sashing strips vertically between the beds in rows one, two, four and five. Pin them right sides together with a 6 mm seam allowance, then machine together.

10  Arrange row three in the same way as step 9, but without sashing on either side of the tree block. Machine and press all the seams.

11  Now insert the 69 cm strips of sashing horizontally between the rows and pin together, matching the corners of the bed block carefully, as even little errors of alignment will look huge. Machine and press as before.

12  Pin the remaining 69 cm sashing strips along the top and bottom. Machine and press, then attach the 94 cm strips to each side. An allowance has been made for little errors in the measurement of these strips, so trim where necessary.

### OUTER BORDER

13  Now cut strips for the outer border: you need two measuring 9 × 102 cm, and two measuring 9 × 127 cm. Pin and sew the shorter strips at top and bottom, then do the same with the longer strips at the sides. Press the seams open and trim as necessary.

### LAYERING

14  Prepare the quilt for layering by pressing all the seams open and cutting off any stray threads. Cut the backing fabric and cotton wadding to size; they should be at least 5 cm bigger all around than the quilt top.

15  Lay the backing fabric on a flat surface, wrong side up, and smooth it out. Secure it at intervals around the edge with masking tape. Place the cotton wadding on top, matching the edges. Place the quilt centrally on top, right side up, and fasten all three layers together with safety pins every 7.5 cm. (Spray fabric adhesive can be used instead of pins – just follow the manufacturer's instructions – but the finished quilt must be washed to remove the glue.)

QUILTING

16  Mandy tends to use a combination of hand- and machine-quilting on her quilts. She advises using a matching or invisible thread (see Tips) to stabilise the quilt by machining in the 'ditch' around the bed blocks and along all the borders.

17  Once the quilt is stabilised, you can start hand-quilting with quilting thread in chunky running stitch. (On mine, this is done as a wavy line around the patterned border.) As it's hard to hide chunky knots at the end of the thread, it's best not to use them at all. Simply put the needle in 2.5 cm away from where you need it, come out at the quilting spot and do a backstitch to hold things tight.

EMBELLISHMENTS

18  If you wish, sew wide ricrac along the outer sashing either by hand or machine. This cuts down on the amount of quilting needed, as does adding buttons between each block.

19  Sew the numbered buttons to just the top sheet on each bed. They should be arranged randomly so that the children have to search for the right date. Of course, 25, for Christmas Day, goes on the bucket. And don't forget to hang the miniature lights on the tree.

20  If you'd like to add a row of bunting above the tree, cut out eight little triangles from scraps of fabric. Position them on the sashing above the tree, pin the narrow ricrac along the top and stitch in place by hand or machine.

BINDING

21  The binding goes around the edge of the quilt, enclosing all the layers. Cut two long strips of binding fabric 2 cm wide and stitch together in one long strip. Press the seam open, then fold the strip in half lengthways and press again.

22  Pin the binding along one side of the quilt, right sides together and raw edges matching. Starting 7.5 cm from the beginning of the binding, and sewing 6 mm from the raw edge, stitch until you reach one corner, stopping 6 mm from the end – this is very important. Lift the needle and pull the work away from the machine, leaving the thread still attached. Fold the binding up and away from you towards the north so that it is aligned with the edge of the quilt. Make sure it is straight.

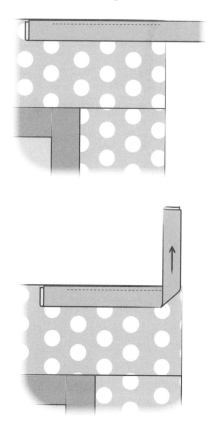

23  Holding the corner, fold the binding back down, south, aligning it with the raw edge. The folded corner must be square. Pin and sew over

the fold, continuing down the next edge. Repeat with the other corners.

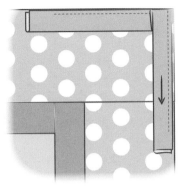

24 When you return to the starting point, turn under 6 mm of the beginning of the binding. Place the end of the binding inside the fold, trim to size, then sew right over the top.

25 Fold the binding over to the back and the corners will miraculously mitre for you on their own. Slipstitch or topstitch in place.

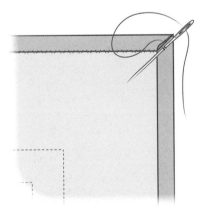

FACES

26 Cut twenty-four 7.5 cm circles from the coloured calico, and twenty-four 4 cm circles from thick wadding.

27 Using a matching thread and a running stitch, hand-sew around the outside of each calico circle about 6 mm from the edge. Place a wadding circle in the middle of each, then pull the thread to gather the fabric around it. The heads should be round and flattish, not scrunched into a ball. When the shape is right, fasten off the thread.

28 Using permanent marker pens, draw a face on each head. You want a variety of expressions – happy, sad, surprised, yawning, sleeping and so on – because they'll make you laugh in years to come. As a final touch, add a little blusher to the cheeks.

HAIR

29 For different hairstyles, cut a group of your chosen threads (whether wool, cotton, raffia, string or mohair) into 7.5 cm lengths, tie them in the middle, then glue or stitch them to the head. The hair can then be styled to your liking – plaited, bunched, arranged in a bun or cut short. Another way of making short styles is to embroider French knots, satin stitch or large loops (see pages 236–7).

30 Decorate the finished hair-dos with narrow ribbons and beads.

HANGING

31 Take the fabric for the sleeve and iron a 6 mm hem along each long side. Fold it over the top of the calendar, leaving an open channel large enough for the pole to go through, then pin in place. Slipstitch by hand along both long edges.

32 Thread the pole through the sleeve and tie a ribbon or string loop to each end. You can use drawing pins to prevent the loops slipping off the pole. Hang the calender somewhere accessible and put a treat inside each little bed.

YLI invisible thread comes in smoke and clear and a large reel lasts for ages. Beware other types, as they can snag on the reel and be a disaster to use.

To give quilting thread extra strength, it helps if you run it through a beeswax candle before stitching.

# SEASON'S GREETINGS

———

## CARDS, TAGS AND WRAPPING

If I had a top five list of things I love in life, it would run something like this: buying clothes for me and my children; cooking; plumping cushions to create the perfect sofa; American quilts; and a pile of beautifully wrapped and attractively labelled Christmas presents.

It's not for nothing that the most expensive brands in the world are known for their exquisite wrapping. If you received an iconic orange Hermès box beautifully wrapped with its trademark ribbon, would you even care what was inside? I've always believed that the way a gift is presented is just as important as the gift itself. After all, it's the first thing someone sees when you hand it over to them. The big brands have proved that gorgeous packaging builds a sense of excitement. So whether you're giving a jar of jelly beans or a pretty mug costing just a couple of pounds, wrapping it beautifully says you care, and the gift is elevated to a whole new level of thoughtfulness.

Gifts have been wrapped since the Chinese invented paper thousands of years ago, but the tradition of Christmas gift-wrap is much more recent. In fact, before Queen Victoria married the German-born Prince Albert in 1840, we hardly knew a thing about Christmas in the UK. By the end of the 19th century,

however, Christmas had become our biggest annual celebration, and presents were wrapped in plain brown paper or tissue.

Needless to say, I do a lot of wrapping, but while I love to make presents look beautiful, it's also crucial to keep the costs down. I tend to buy a giant roll of heavy-duty brown craft paper online or from the Post Office, which can cost as little as £5.99 for 25 metres. The other bargain basement and hugely effective wrapping I use is old newspaper. Using old copies of the FT or fashion and interiors magazines to wrap gifts is very effective. One thing I wouldn't be without is a Sellotape dispenser you can wear around your hand or wrist. It's a marvellous invention and has saved me literally hours when wrapping presents.

Since my paper is cheap, I do spend a bit more on embellishing, and throughout the year I keep my eyes peeled for bargain ribbon. It's pretty easy to achieve a Christmassy feel without having a particularly Christmassy ribbon. Tartan works brilliantly, as does red, gold, purple or any jewel colour. A couple of years ago I found metres and metres of red gingham ribbon for a steal, which I paired with plain brown paper for everyone's Christmas presents, and the combination looked really smart. The following year, however, I struggled to make the pale yellow ribbon I had look festive. In retrospect, I should have kept it for Easter. My obsession with ribbon means that I have a pretty big collection at my disposal, but I am very careful with it. I trial-wrap the ribbon around my gifts

and tie my bows before cutting the ribbons so I have minimal wastage. If you prefer a more relaxed approach, cut roughly six and a bit times the length of your present as that is usually enough to wrap around the gift and tie a good bow. This chapter includes bow-tying techniques and gorgeous ideas for embellishing, courtesy of wrapping queen Jane Means.

My red gingham ribbon and brown paper combo is a perfect example of my obsession for neatness and themes. Every year, all my presents match and have a really strong theme so everyone knows they're from me, even if the tag falls off under the tree and I'm not there. Obviously, some gifts are really special and these are the ones you might want to make look as good as an Hermès box. If you want to push the boat out, try the fabulous paper marbling on page 61. It's definitely one of the most beautiful crafts ever. For really small gifts, I wrap them like crackers, using tissue paper and tying ribbons round the ends. And for the children's stocking fillers, I buy loads of cheap Christmas paper – the type you get in pound shops – and wind tons of cheap sticky tape around it. This takes them ages to open on Christmas morning and builds a wonderful sense of suspense.

When it comes to Christmas cards I have to confess to copping out. I love to receive cards, but I hardly ever send them. My lame excuse is not having a proper list of addresses for all my friends. However, I received a brilliant email card last year and was considering sending one of those in future until it was politely pointed out that the dancing elves email is very well known, even old hat, so bang

went that idea. I feel bad about not sending cards to everyone, but I don't claim to be perfect. I devote hours to personalising my gifts, but if I were to send cards as well, I'd lose weeks of my life as I'd want to handmake and personalise every single one. I've therefore narrowed it down to sending cards to close family members and people I see regularly. If you're into handmaking cards, my advice is to limit the number of folk you send them to and avoid any situations where someone might see your thoughtful, handmade creation on a mantelpiece and wonder where theirs is. I hang the cards I receive all around the house, and save them to make other things with. There's a great card-hanging project on page 74 to help you display yours beautifully.

Last year I received a Christmas card-cum-present that is so lovely I'm going to have it framed. It is a 1950s' telegram, bought blank, with my name written on it in the loveliest calligraphy. I was absolutely thrilled with it. Through my research for this book, I've since found out that the telegram cost £5, and having previously used Claire Gould of Calligraphy for Weddings, I know that the services of a calligrapher for work of this quality would be about £20 – not bad for something that I will treasure forever. If you fancy sending this sort of wonderful telegram, you can try finding a local calligrapher or someone who will work by post, or even try local tattoo artists, who often do really cool stuff. And if you're feeling very artistic, you could have a go yourself as there are plenty of calligraphy courses out there.

# EMBOSSED CARD

You might have noticed that there's a snowflake theme running through this book. Not only are snowflakes incredibly visual and Christmassy, they're also the sign of a charity appeal that's very close to my heart. You can read all about Home-Start UK and the Snowflake Appeal on page 244. The beautiful embossed snowflake card shown here was designed by Clare Pentlow.

## *YOU WILL NEED*

---

Ink pad (clear embossing stamp pad) · Snowflake rubber stamp, or you can have your own designs made into stamps · 1 sheet white card, 2 types of pearlescent card and 1 sheet silver card, or whatever colours and textures you like (you can also use leftover wrapping paper or wallpaper) · Silver embossing powder · Heatproof mat · Heat tool · Pencil and compass · Craft knife and cutting mat (better than scissors) · Double-sided tape · Sticky foam pads, for mounting · Metal ruler · Ready-made blank cards, folded size 12 × 12 cm

1  Ink the rubber stamp and press it onto a sheet of white card. Cover the snowflake image with embossing powder and tap off the excess. Place the card on a heatproof mat. Holding a heat gun about 8 cm from the card surface, heat the powder until it has melted. Repeat this step with a piece of pearlescent card.

2  Using a pencil and compass, draw a circle around the embossed snowflake on the pearlescent card and cut around it.

3  Draw a slightly larger circle on another piece of card and cut around it. Attach the pearlescent snowflake to it with double-sided tape.

4  Take the embossed piece of white card and draw a circle around the centre of the design, which is small enough to fit in the centre of the embossed snowflake. Cut out the snowflake design, place a sticky foam pad on the back and press it to the middle of the snowflake.

5  Cut out a 9 × 9 cm square of white card. Cut out a slightly bigger square of shiny silver card. (I used blue silver for contrast) Stick the white card to the silver card using double-sided tape. Attach this to the front of a ready-made card using more tape.

6  Attach the circular snowflake to the centre front of the card using sticky foam pads.

*You can layer up the design as much as you want with different types and colours of paper.*

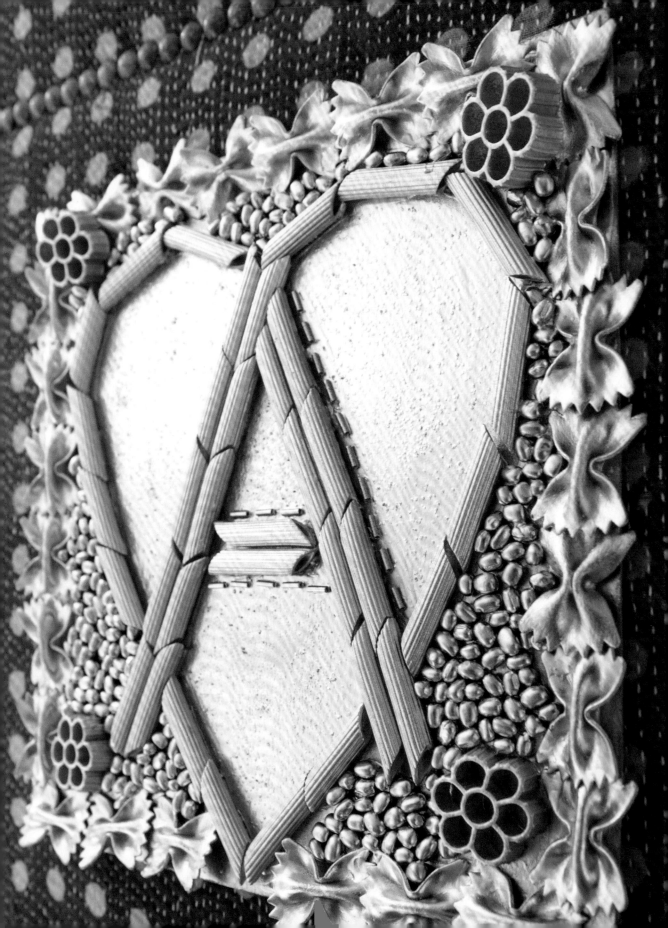

# GOLDEN PASTA CARD

If you're anything like me, making a pasta card will bring memories of school crafts flooding back. However, designer and illustrator Poppy Chancellor has come up with a chic gold spray design that's a world away from anything I ever made at school.

      This is a great project to do with children, and I did debate whether it actually belongs in the children's chapter, but then I worried that grown-ups might not take it seriously. All I know is that if I received a handmade card like this, I'd be absolutely thrilled. So you 'midas' well have a go!

## *YOU WILL NEED*

-----------

Pencil and metal ruler • A4 sheet of thick card or mounting board (something sturdy to hold the weight of the pasta) • Bone folder (similar to a paper knife but made of bone) • Pasta in various shapes and sizes • Dried beans or peas • PVA glue and paintbrush • Sequins and glitter (optional) • Gold spray

1 Make a pencil mark at the top and bottom of the A4 card where it will be folded. Hold a metal ruler beside the marks, then run a bone folder alongside the ruler to score a straight line. Keeping the scored line on the outside, fold the card in half. This technique prevents the card from cracking where it shouldn't.

2 Draw an outline design on one side of the card so that you have a strong shape to follow for the next step.

3 Start placing pasta shapes, beans and peas around the design, and once you're happy with the arrangement, stick it in place with PVA glue. If you like, you can add further embellishments, such as sequins and glitter. Set aside to dry. This will take a couple of hours.

4 Holding the gold spray about 15–20 cm away from the card, spray the whole design, then set it aside to dry.

-----------

*Initials are a great way to personalise cards. Poppy made the 'A' card in the photo opposite for her mum.*

-----------

# FABRIC WINDOW CARD

The Christmas card was invented in the 1840s when Henry Cole, pioneer of the penny post and founder of the V&A Museum in London, commissioned an artist to design a card that depicted a group of people having Christmas dinner. Ready-made cards went on to become widely available, but they were expensive to buy, so children, including Queen Victoria's, were encouraged to make their own. I'm all for keeping up the habit of hand-making cards, and I'm particularly fond of the design shown here, mainly because it can be personalised with favourite fabrics.

## *YOU WILL NEED*

Tracing paper and pencil · Sheet of card · Cutting mat and craft knife · Ready-made card, folded size 15 × 15 cm · Scissors (preferably pinking shears to prevent fraying) · Fabric · Double-sided tape · Ruler

1  Trace around the bauble, tree or star template on page 229–31, transfer to the sheet of card and cut out neatly with a craft knife.

2  Open the ready-made card, put the template on the front and draw around it. Put the card on the mat and cut around the outline.

3  Cut a piece of fabric big enough to cover the shape you've cut out but smaller than the card. Using double-sided tape, stick the fabric on the inside of the card.

4  Cut a 14.5 cm square of card and stick it over the fabric with double-sided tape. The card is now ready for your greeting.

*You can adapt this technique for gift tags. Cut pieces of card measuring 15 × 5 cm and fold in three. Trace the tree on page 230 and scale it down on a photocopier. Transfer to card, as in step 1, place it on the middle section of the tri-fold card and follow steps 2 and 3. Fold the left side over the middle and stick down with double-sided tape. Punch a hole in the top left-hand corner and thread cotton or narrow ribbon through it.*

# OVEN-BAKED GIFT TAGS

Very few people have time to make all their presents. I know I don't. However, there are lots of little ways to personalise gifts, and here it's with oven-baked clay gift tags.

This is a great kitchen table craft that you can involve the children in, or just do on your own. The lucky recipient can save the tag as a little extra present in itself.

## *YOU WILL NEED*

---

Oven-bake clay (e.g. Fimo or Sculpey) • 1 large ceramic tile
Rolling pin • Small biscuit cutters, up to 5 cm in diameter • Solid metal
letter stamps • Knitting needle • Acrylic paint • Paintbrush • Wire brush,
scouring sponge or rag • String, narrow ribbon or wire

1 Preheat the oven to the temperature recommended by the clay manufacturers.

2 Break off a piece of clay about the size of a golf ball and soften it with your fingers. Place it on the tile and roll out to a thickness of about 1 cm. Using your cutters, stamp various shapes.

3 Use the letter stamps to impress a name or message onto each piece of clay. Don't press too hard or you will distort the shape.

4 Using a knitting needle, make a hole in each piece of clay through which string or ribbon can be threaded later.

5 Place the tags, still on the ceramic tile, in the oven and bake for the time advised in the instructions on the clay wrapping.

6 Allow the baked tags to cool, then apply a thin layer of acrylic paint. Set aside to dry.

7 Using a wire brush, slightly dampened scouring sponge or rag, rub off most of the paint so that it's mainly within the impressed letters. This gives a brilliant distressed look to your tags.

8 Thread some string, ribbon or wire through each hole and tie the tags to your presents.

---

*This craft can also be used to make lovely Christmas tree decorations.*

---

# MARBLED PAPER

The kaleidoscope of intricate colours found on marbled papers never fails to take my breath away. I've loved this craft since I first tried it at school, and there is a plethora of ways you can use it at Christmas time: cards, gift tags, fancy envelopes, very special wrapping paper, gift boxes, beautiful notebooks, pictures and even napkin rings. Something else I've seen that looks sensational (although not really for Christmas) is to use it as wallpaper in a small room, such as a loo, or to line bookcases. I'd put marbled paper everywhere if I could.

Kate Brett of Payhembury Marbling has been creating the most exquisite papers for more than 30 years. She's enthralled by the history of her craft and collects old papers and references to reproduce traditional designs. Marbling is not an exact science: only time and experience will teach you to judge the correct quantities and proportions of the ingredients for each marbling task. Kate says she still has ups and downs when creating her papers, so don't lose your marbles too soon when making yours.

Before you get stuck in, let me explain the process. Traditional marbling uses water-based paints, such as gouache, watercolours or acrylics. If water-based paints or gouache are used, the paper to be marbled is first sponged with a solution of alum, which acts as a mordant (bond) for the colour. If using acrylic paints, you don't need to do this. Almost any paper can be used, though some papers are easier to handle than others. Colour is then floated on the surface of a liquid before being drawn into patterns with a stick or comb. If the pattern is to be controlled and not just accidental, the liquid must have a greater viscosity than that of water. For that reason, a soup or 'size', as it's called, is made from a seaweed called carrageen. The size has just the right viscosity to allow the colours floating on the surface to be drawn gently into a pattern without sinking them. It's clever stuff, capable of retaining every single detail of the most delicate and complex patterns. Things other than carrageen, such as wallpaper paste or gelatine, can also be used to make a size, but these are more suitable when using oil-based paints.

You can use the traditional water-based paints, or you can make your own colours using pigment ground with gum arabic. Simply mix 1 teaspoon paint from a tube with 2 tablespoons water until it has a milky consistency. To apply the paint to the size, dip a brush in the colour and shake or tap it over the surface without actually touching it.

# YOU WILL NEED

———

Dried carrageen seaweed (available from healthfood shops or specialist suppliers) or powdered carrageenan (more expensive but much less required; available online) · Colander · Fine muslin or a jelly bag, for straining · Blender · Bucket · Powdered alum (available from chemists) · Paper, e.g. cartridge, drawing or handmade papers (avoid those with too much calcium carbonate, which makes them shiny and non-absorbent) · Rubber gloves · Sponge · Pressing boards (must be larger than the paper you're marbling) · Marbling inks (watercolours, gouache or acrylic paints) · Jars or pots, for mixing colours · Cheap 10 mm paintbrushes or pastry brushes · Eye dropper · Ox gall (available in art shops) or watered-down washing-up liquid · Plastic tray, at least 375 × 250 mm and 50–75 mm deep · Newspaper strips, cut to the same width as the tray · Small piece of wood (optional) · Knitting needle · Combs (see Tips) · String · Soft beeswax and cloth

### MAKING THE SIZE

1 If using dried caragEen, put 28 g of it into a large saucepan with 2 litres of water. Bring slowly to the boil and let it boil for 1–3 minutes, stirring constantly. Add 2 litres of cold water, then strain through a colander and discard the seaweed. Strain again through fine muslin. Leave to stand in a cool place for at least 12 hours or overnight. The liquid should be like a very thin jelly. Strain again through fine muslin to make it completely smooth.

If using powdered carrageenan, nearly fill a blender with warm water, add 5 teaspoons of the powder and whiz together. Transfer the liquid to a bucket. Repeat this step with another 5 teaspoons of the powder and add to the bucket. Top up with enough warm water to half-fill the bucket and leave overnight.

### PREPARING THE PAPER

2 Add 50 g powdered alum to 600 ml warm water, stir and leave to stand for 15 minutes at room temperature.

3 Place a sheet of paper on a board. Wearing rubber gloves, dip the sponge in the alum, squeeze out the excess and sponge evenly over the paper. Place another sheet of paper on top of the sponged sheet and apply alum in the same way. Continue to alum as many sheets as you wish to marble. Cover with a board and leave for a few hours before using.

### PREPARING THE PATTERN

4 Put 1 teaspoon of your first chosen colour from a tube into a jar and mix well with about 2 tablespoons water. Use the eye dropper to add 2 drops of ox gall to reduce the surface tension and help it to spread. Further colours will need more ox gall. Stir well.

5 Pour a 2.5 cm depth of the size into the marbling tray. It should be liquid, not a jelly, and at roughly room temperature; it may be two or three degrees cooler than that, but must not be warmer. If the size is too cold, add a little warm water. If it is too thick, add a little water.

6 In order to get rid of bubbles, which will prevent the colour spreading, skim the complete surface of the size by drawing a strip of newspaper down the tray. It's also important to do this if the size has been standing for more than 30 seconds because it acquires a skin that will also affect the colour absorption.

7 Immediately after skimming, stir the prepared colour and dip a clean brush in it. To make a traditional combed pattern, the colours should be applied in vertical rows from the top to the bottom of the tray. Wipe off the excess paint against the edge of the jar, then shake it over the size or tap it against the jar or a piece of wood held in your empty hand. You are essentially splashing it onto the surface. The drops should spread 2.5 cm or more. If they spread and shrink, the size is colder than the colour, so add a little warm water, mixing well but taking care not to make any bubbles. Skim the size as in step 6 and test the paint again.

If the colour does *not* spread in the first instance, stir 2 more drops of ox gall into the paint. Skim the size as in step 6 and test the paint again. There's a fair bit of bit of trial and error involved here, especially if it's your first time at marbling. If the colour still does not spread, the size is too thick. Thin it with water, mixing well but taking care not to make any bubbles. It should be just thick enough to allow you to draw the pattern.

8 To add a second colour, prepare it as in step 4, but it will require more ox gall than the first colour if it is to spread to the same extent. Apply it with a clean brush as before, shaking it on top or beside the first colour.

Do not be in too much of a hurry to try three colours, as it takes lots of practice to work more than two colours together and balance them with ox gall so that they do not wash off the sheet. As previously, a third colour requires more ox gall than the second colour.

Paints can be mixed together to make different colours, and they can also be diluted with water if they become too thick or you want to make them paler. Just make sure they are thoroughly mixed and use more ox gall as dilution increases the volume of colour.

9  Before starting this step, remember that the colours are only a thin film floating on the surface of the size, and any violent movement will make them sink, so work very gently. Take a knitting needle and draw it backwards and forwards across the rows of paint to make horizontal lines of colour. Then take a comb and draw it carefully down the tray so that a recognisable combed pattern appears. You can then add curls to this with a more widely spaced comb.

PAPER MEETS PAINT

10  Choose a prepared sheet of paper, which is still damp from the alum but not wet. If it is wet, it will not pick up the colour, and if it is too dry, it will be difficult to lay down on the size. Lift it, alum side down, by diagonally opposite corners – top left-hand corner in the left hand, bottom right-hand corner in the right hand. Hold the hands close together so that the sheet hangs in the form of a U. Lower the left-hand corner onto the size but do not let go, then slowly lower the right hand to lay the whole sheet down. The aim is to avoid trapping any air between the paper and the size because air bubbles prevent the sheet from touching the colour and thus leave a blank space.

11  As soon as the paper is floating (just a few seconds), pull it over the edge of the tray by the two corners closest to you so that the excess size jelly is scraped off and returned to the tray. Don't worry, the paint has already soaked into the paper, so that won't come off too.

12  To make further sheets of marbled paper, skim the size as in step 6, making sure you remove all the floating paint. Some paint will sink, so the size will become dirtier as the day goes on, but as long as you skim the surface every time you use it, the result will be fine. Repeat steps 7–11.

13  Hang the marbled sheets to dry on lines of string, then iron them flat with a dry iron. Polishing the surface with soft beeswax will enhance the colours and preserve the pattern.

---

*Size works well for marbling at a room temperature of 15°C/60°F. It is not workable if it is too cold (10°C/50°F), nor if it is too warm (20°C/70°F or so). The temperature of the size should be approximately the same as that of the paints and combs. If kept in a cool place, size will retain its viscosity for 2–3 days.*

*Combed patterns can be made by using a plastic hair comb from which you have broken off alternate teeth. Alternatively, place a row of panel pins or toothpicks along the edge of very strong card or millboard (the spacing is up to you), glue them firmly in place and paint with varnish to make them waterproof.*

*As a rule, the fewer the colours used and the less a pattern is combed, the brighter the pattern will be, unless you're an expert.*

*If you'd like to learn more about marbling, there's an interesting film about it at www.eafa.org.uk/catalogue/7747. There is also further advice at www.edenworkshops.com/Paper_Marbling_-_A_Free_Manual_to_Download.html.*

*You can also search online for local marbling workshops.*

---

# GIFT-WRAPPING IDEAS

You probably know by now that beautiful gift-wrapping comes pretty high on my Christmas agenda. I admit to having a vast collection of paper, ribbon and tagging fodder that I keep in an old vintage suitcase, which I had specially compartmentalised. Brown paper tends to be my staple wrapping, but I also use newspaper and magazines. Ribbon is where I spend the most money, but it is possible to get good deals if you buy at sale time, second-hand or in bulk. I also save and reuse all the ribbon I receive on gifts.

Recently I came across the extraordinary wrapping talents of Jane Means, also known as the 'Gift-Wrap Guru'. Jane has wrapped for Selfridges, Ralph Lauren and *Country Living Magazine*; she has even wrapped a gift for Her Majesty the Queen. People travel from all over the world to attend Jane's wrapping courses. There's just about nothing she can't make look like a million dollars, and, luckily for us, she's shared a few of her wrapping secrets here.

---

## WRAPPING WITH PLEATED PAPER

Jane first came across paper pleating on a trip to Japan. There's a country that really knows how to wrap. This idea makes a simple box look much more interesting.

YOU WILL NEED
- Sheet of wrapping paper
- Double-sided tape
- Scissors

1 Fold a sheet of wrapping paper in half, ensuring that the sides are even and straight, then open it out again.

2 Grasp the crease with the finger and thumb of both hands about a third of the way in from the sides and pinch along it to make a pleat no deeper than 2 cm. Fold it away from you.

3 Lift the paper up and tuck the top part underneath so that the doubled paper above the first pleat is the same depth as the pleat. Make sure the sides are straight, then press down in the middle and slide your hands out to the sides to make a crease.

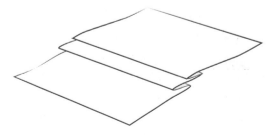

4  Open out the paper again, and grasp the crease as before and fold it away from you to form a second pleat.

5  Repeat steps 3 and 4 to make a few more pleats. Turn the paper over and tape the pleats together to hold them in place.

6  Place the paper on top of the gift with the pleats running lengthways and decide where you want them to sit – either in the middle or off-centre. Gently crease the paper along two opposite sides, then turn the paper over to the wrong side and the creases will show you where to position the gift to keep the pleats in the right place. Fold under one raw long edge and stick it down with a piece of double-sided tape at a slight angle. Overlap the paper from both sides, then peel the backing paper off the double-sided tape and stick down.

7  Fold down the pleated paper at one end of the gift, then tuck in the corners to make a triangular shape. Turn in the raw edge of the paper, then fold it over the end of the gift. Repeat this with the other end, then use double-sided tape close to the edge to fasten it.

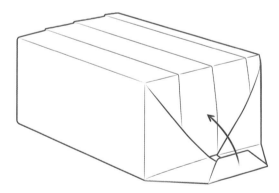

*Twigs, feathers, foliage, holly and berries can be attached to gifts with a glue gun.*

*Write on fresh leaves with a metallic gel pen and use them as gift tags. This works well with ivy, bay and laurel.*

*If a gift has a really awkward shape, try wrapping it in a vintage silk scarf instead of paper.*

# WRAPPING CIRCULAR ITEMS

Here's a nifty way of wrapping something like a round tin of biscuits.

**YOU WILL NEED**
- Biscuit tin
- Sheet of wrapping paper
- Scissors
- Double-sided tape
- Embellishments, such as ribbons, moss, walnuts, berries, holly

1  Place the tin on a sheet of wrapping paper, roll it one revolution, add 5 cm and cut it to length. Now measure the width of the paper so it comes just over halfway above the middle of the tin on both top and bottom, add 5 cm for overlap and cut to size.

2  Fold in about 2 cm at one short end of the paper and put a piece of double-sided tape in the middle, overlapping the edge, to hold it down. Now roll the wrapping paper around the tin and stick it together.

3  Casually fold the paper over the top of the tin (you will do it properly later) and sit the tin on that end. Wrapping proper must *always* start with the underside of the item.

4 Fold one point of the paper into the centre of the tin, then make 1 cm pleats in the paper all the way around, ensuring that they always point to the middle. (Small pleats distract the eye and make any mistakes less obvious.) Keep a finger in the centre all the time to avoid going off course.

5 When you get to the end, you will notice a little fan of paper in the middle. Trim this off, fold the final flap over it neatly (this might need trimming too) and secure with several bits of double-sided tape.

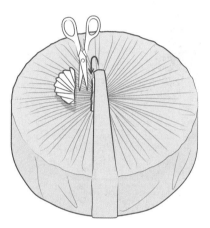

6 Repeat the pleating on the other side of the tin, then embellish the top of the wrapping with whatever you wish.

---

*If you're using ribbon patterned on only one side, twist it as necessary for the pattern to show before tightening it.*

*Once you've perfected the technique for tying bows, you can try attaching them with wire to Christmas baubles to hang on your tree.*

*To attach pine cones to your gift embellishments, tie thin ribbon around the stem, then tie the ribbon to the gift. Cones can be sprayed gold to look extra Christmassy.*

---

# THE PERFECT BOW

Learning to tie the perfect bow is one of life's light-bulb moments.

**YOU WILL NEED**
- Length of ribbon
- Scissors

1 With your ribbon wrapped once round your gift, hold both ends together to ensure they are the same length.

2 Tie a single knot and make the first loop for a bow. Now, going in the opposite direction to the one you usually take to make a bow, take the ribbon for the second loop to the left and around the first loop. Feed it through the back from the left and tighten the bow.

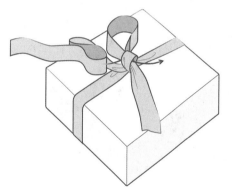

# FLAT BOW

This style of bow is perfect for dressing anything flat or fragile, such as gift vouchers or the Christmas cake on page 181.

YOU WILL NEED
- Reversible ribbon
- Double-sided tape
- Scissors

1  Cut a piece of ribbon to the width of three fingers. Stick the same length of double-sided tape to the back and peel off the paper. Set aside.

2  Stick a small piece of double-sided tape to the end of ribbon still attached to the reel and peel off the paper. Fold the ribbon back on itself to form a circle and stick it down.

3  Pinch the circle in the middle, place it on a flat surface and stick the small bit of ribbon at right angles across the centre. Tuck the ends behind the back and stick down.

4  Only now do you cut the ribbon off the reel, but first measure how much you need to wrap around your gift with a slight overlap. Cut a piece of double-sided tape a little shorter than the bow, stick it on the back and peel off the paper. Wrap the ribbon around your gift and stick the bow to it.

---

*Adding a few fresh herbs, such as lavender, rosemary or bay leaves, to your embellishment not only looks great, but smells amazing too.*

*Use any broken or unwanted costume jewellery to brighten up your gift-wrap. A diamanté brooch will really add sparkle.*

*Use old magazines and photocopy sheet music to make bows and interesting wrapping paper.*

---

# RIBBON ROSES

I'm a big fan of ribbon roses. You can attach them to gifts in a cluster to resemble a little bouquet and it looks really pretty.

YOU WILL NEED
- Wire-edged ribbon
- Pins (optional)
- Needle and thread

1  Pull 10mm of wire from one side of the ribbon and secure by bending it backwards or poking the end through the ribbon.

2  Gather the ribbon along the side where you pulled the wire. It will curl as you do so.

3  To create the centre of the flower, roll up one end of the ribbon as tightly as you can. As the flower gets bigger, bend the ribbon outwards and further away from the centre. You can adjust the shape as you go and pin it together if you like.

4  Once the whole piece of ribbon is rolled up, sew together at the back of the flower shape to hold it in place, making sure you stitch the centre tightly to maintain its shape.

# CARDHOLDER

Having somewhere to hang the Christmas cards you receive is really useful, and Mandy Shaw's beautiful, big bow cardholder is a joy. You can make several of these and hang them around your home.

## *YOU WILL NEED*

---

56 × 46 cm piece of tartan fabric • Scissors • Tape measure • 14 × 22 cm piece of cotton wadding • Pins • Sewing machine and suitable thread • Knitting needle • Hand-sewing needle • Tailor's chalk • 1 metre of 2.5 cm tape • 1 D-ring • 10 cm square of gold fabric • Button or brooch • Small gold safety pins • Paper clips

**A 6 mm seam allowance has been added to all measurements.**

1  Lay out the tartan and cut a lengthways strip 16 cm wide (this is for the tails of the bow). Now cut two tartan rectangles measuring 14 × 22 cm (for the bow itself).

2  The bow is padded, so place the two tartan rectangles right sides together and lay them on top of the wadding. Pin well, then machine all the way around the edge, leaving a 5 cm gap in the middle of one long side. Snip off the corners and turn the right way out via the gap. Poke out the corners with a knitting needle and hand-sew the gap closed.

3  Fold the long strip in half, right sides together. Using tailor's chalk, mark a spot 5 cm down the raw edge and draw a line from that spot to the nearest folded corner. Cut along the line to create a point. Do the same at the opposite end.

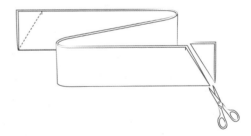

4  Machine around the raw edges of the strip, leaving a 5 cm gap in the middle of one side. Snip off the points and turn the right way out via the gap. Poke out the corners with a knitting needle and hand-sew the gap closed.

5 Thread one end of the tape through the D-ring and make a few stitches to hold it in place. Hem the opposite end of the tape.

6 Fold the gold fabric into quarters and cut a curve on the raw-edged sides to create a rough circle. Hand-sew with running stitch around the circle about 1 cm from the edge. Gently pull the thread to gather the circle into a puff and fasten off with a backstitch.

7 Pinch the long sides of the padded tartan together in the middle and stitch the gathers together at the back. Fold the strip for the tails in half and sew the folded end to the back of the bow. Sew the tape to the back of the bow, positioning the D-ring slightly above it.

8 Finally, sew the gold puff to the front of the bow with a sparkly button, or pin a brooch in the middle of the puff.

9 To use the holder, pin small gold safety pins to the back of the tape at regular intervals so only little brass bars show at the front. Suspend the holder by the D-ring, then attach your cards by clipping them to the brass bars with paper clips.

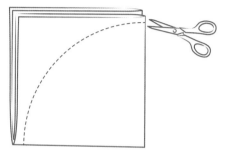

# THE CHRISTMAS TABLE

—

*PLANNING, PREPARATION*
*AND PIZZAZZ*

If you think organising the Christmas Day celebrations is a piece of cake, you're in the minority. Most people hosting lunch for a big crowd find it pretty overwhelming. My secret to making sure the biggest event of the year goes without a hitch is, wait for it . . . careful organisation and planning.

When it comes to the Christmas table, my biggest consideration is the food. After all, what is the point of a beautifully decked-out table if you can't fit the turkey or sprouts on it? Planning your space before you get carried away with extravagant decorations is key. You have to consider whether your table is wide enough to take the food going down the middle along with whatever decorations you've planned. If your table won't accommodate all the food or you want to prioritise the decorations, a sturdy trestle table does a great job of holding whatever the main table won't.

It will come as no surprise to anyone who knows me that I like my table to be glittery. By that, I mean decked with an abundance of candles and tinsel. I sort of throw everything at it and when it's done I look at it and love it.

My tip is to have a box that you can start filling up in advance of the day with the things you want to use to decorate the room and the table. That way, when it comes to setting everything up, you're not wrestling with the table as well as the

bird in the kitchen. Everything will be right there and you won't be searching out the correct tablecloth, ironing napkins, or looking for candles to go in the candlesticks. If your box is organised enough, you could even give the job of laying and decorating the table to someone else who might be sitting with their feet up. Delegation, delegation, delegation. Get everyone involved.

I believe you never need to buy anything specifically for your Christmas table. I tend to use my everyday things and enhance them with Christmassy bits and pieces. Of course, there's always an exception, and mine is special Christmas napkins that I made with the Tavistock Embroiderers' Guild a few Christmases ago. These come out every year and I absolutely love them. If you'd like to make a set, see page 84.

Thin tinsel (it always comes back to tinsel with me) is brilliant for decorating candlesticks and tying around napkins or crackers, and a glass bowl or storm lantern filled with Christmas baubles is so easy to do and can look really striking. Cast your eye around your home and gather the things you can dress up to make really Christmassy. Think about using evergreen branches and holly or red poinsettias that you'll find in abundance at garden stores to bring Christmas to your dining area.

My other big Christmas essential is gold spray. You can make anything look festive with gold spray. Try spraying walnuts or pine cones and some dried hydrangeas and popping them in a vase. I've also been known to cover fruit in

edible gold spray. There's absolutely no doubt that gold spray comes very close to matching my passion for glitter.

Candles are without doubt one of the easiest ways to decorate any celebration table, and I always have them at Christmas. The soft glow of candlelight brings a certain ambience that really can't be reproduced with other types of lighting. There are essentially three different types of candle: votives (such as tea-lights in glass containers); pillar candles (much chunkier and can stand without support); and tapers (tall, thin candles in lots of different heights). Decorating your table with candles in a mixture of shapes and sizes is a great way to add interest. One of my favourites, which I got a few years ago, is a Swedish Angel Chimes candle that twinkles as the heat rises and spins the angel on top. I use two of these at Christmas, along with taper candles and votives. There is a great candle project for a very chic set of striped dinner candles by expert candle-maker David Constable on page 87.

When it comes to flowers, I'm a big fan of having a few dainty arrangements in old crystal vases dotted along the table. (You can pick up crystal or clear glass vases incredibly cheaply at charity shops if you haven't any at home.) Small flower arrangements let you see the person sitting opposite you, and they are easy to fit around the food. If you want some inspiration, see Kitten Grayson's beautiful arrangement of Christmas roses on page 96.

I confess I'm not a fan of table runners, but I know I'm alone in this, so I won't fight anyone's desire to have them. However, I do love tablecloths, and, like my napkins, I admit to having one or two special Christmas cloths. They're not just brought out on the day itself – they're used over the whole Christmas period, from early December until New Year. I really like to have that 'feel' of Christmas whenever anyone comes over, and because everyone gathers in our kitchen, I always make sure my table feels festive. Red is a great colour for a Christmas tablecloth, and when you add flowers, poinsettias, evergreens or a bit of tinsel, it always looks ready to party. Just sit the Christmas cake on the table and you have a sure-fire winner if anyone pops round for tea.

On Christmas Day we always have crackers. Much as I love them, I rarely win the cracker-pulling contest, but they're still great fun. If we don't make them from scratch, we buy the ones that you can add your own gifts to and then embellish in appealing ways. There is a brilliant, easy-to-do cracker project on page 99 by the designer Clare Hutchison of Froufrou & Thomas.

I hope you enjoy the projects in this chapter and have a really fantastic Christmas. My checklist opposite will help you to plan your table in advance and make life much easier.

## KIRSTIE'S CHRISTMAS TABLE CHECKLIST

○ Tablecloth, washed and ironed (you might need two if the food is arranged on a separate trestle table)

○ Napkins, washed and ironed

○ Placemats

○ Place settings (see page 90)

○ Chairs (do you have enough for everyone?)

○ Dinner plates

○ Serving bowls (check you have enough for the carrots, sprouts and roast potatoes – if having lots of people, you might need several bowls of each veg on the table)

○ Small bowls for serving accompaniments such as bread sauce and cranberry sauce

○ Meat serving plate (you can buy lovely serving plates second-hand, whether on eBay or in charity shops)

○ Carving knife, fork and sharpener

○ Cutlery

○ Glassware: for wine, water, champagne

○ Water jugs

○ Candlesticks or candelabra

○ Candles (see page 87)

○ Table decorations

○ Crackers (see page 99)

○ Salt and pepper pots

○ Ice bucket and plenty of ice for the cocktails on page 187

# HAND-EMBROIDERED NAPKINS

A few years ago I had the huge privilege of being taught to embroider at Hatfield House, a magnificent stately home in Hertfordshire. I don't think I could have found a more inspirational setting. What's more, my tutors were of the highest calibre: they were Fran Baigent, Karyl Cragg and Brenda Poynter of the Tavistock Embroiderers' Guild. They showed me how to free-hand embroider Christmas napkins, and here I pass on their wisdom and wonderful design.

Embroidery is a centuries-old tradition, and at one time girls like Lady Mary of the TV period drama *Downton Abbey* were obliged to learn the art of needlework to prove they were a good marriage prospect. I'd quite happily master needlework to prove myself to Matthew Crawley any day.

Textile artist Karyl came up with a pretty triangle design to represent a Christmas tree with a little star on top, and once the basic hand-drawn plan was in place, the ladies and I went 'freestyle'. The trick is to make sure your napkin is super-taut in the hoop so that your embroidery stays straight. But my favourite piece of advice, from Brenda, was that my thread should be no longer than from the tip of the middle finger to the elbow because that allows the perfect arm movement when you're stitching.

There are countless embroidery stitches, and you can work the patterns on your tree in any of them you like. If you're a beginner, I suggest you follow the stitch illustrations on pages 236–7.

## *YOU WILL NEED*

Fine, sharp and hard pencil • Cardboard for templates • Ruler and craft knife • Paper • Set of white table napkins (as many as your number of guests) • Embroidery hoop • Tissue paper • Pins • Tacking thread and needle • Good-quality, dye-fast embroidery thread (Fran's tip is to wet a couple lengths of thread and press them between sheets of kitchen paper; if the colour doesn't bleed, the thread is fine to use.) • Fine crewel needle

1 To make a tree template, draw a triangle with an 86 mm base and 114 mm sides on the cardboard. Cut it out with a craft knife.

2 The stitching is worked quite freely and each napkin can be different, so it's best to plan the designs before you start. Using the template,

draw some triangles on a piece of paper and sketch out what you want to embroider. One of our designs looked like this:

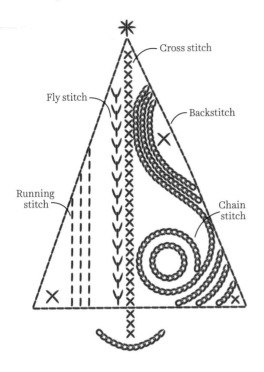

3  Iron a napkin to ensure it's smooth, then place it on your work surface. Position the template diagonally at one corner, the point of the tree facing the centre of the napkin. Place the outer ring of the embroidery hoop over the template to check that it's in the centre of the ring and not too near the corner. Once it's perfectly positioned, remove the hoop.

4  Hold the template firmly in place and draw around it with a hard, very sharp pencil (a soft one might smudge the fabric). The pencil lines will wash off.

5  Centre the triangle outline in the embroidery hoop, making sure the fabric is taut and wrinkle-free. You should be able to tap it like a tambourine.

6  If you want to mark your design on the napkin, trace it onto tissue paper and pin the tracing to the tree outline on the fabric. Using a tacking thread that will show up, make small

tacking stitches along the lines of the design. When all the lines are tacked, carefully tear away the tissue, leaving the tacking in place. It can be removed as you stitch or when the embroidery is complete.

7  To start stitching, always work a couple of tiny stitches on the design line where they will be hidden by subsequent stitching. To finish a thread, weave it through the back of previously worked stitches, or make a couple of tiny backstitches under previous stitching. (It's important that all stitching is well secured because the napkins will have to be laundered.) With these points in mind, start by stitching the outline of the tree using running stitch or stem stitch. For other parts of the design, try out different stitches, such as double knot stitch or Pekinese stitch (see pages 236–7).

---

*Use a thread colour that matches your colour scheme. Metallic thread works well on dark napkins.*

*Start simply, with something like chain stitch, then build up your repertoire of stitches as you get more confident.*

---

# CHRISTMAS CANDLES

It doesn't get more stylish than striped, tapered candles on your Christmas table. If you've made them yourself, they'll definitely be a talking point – and while I think about it, they'd also make a brilliant present.

I asked master candle-maker David Constable to come up with a simple striped design that can easily be achieved at home, and he did me proud. You can buy the appliqué wax strips in lots of different colours, and they look so smart when mixed with votive and pillar candles placed along the table.

David, who taught me how to make candles for my house in Devon, has been practising his craft for more than sixty years, so he's a true master. His wax creations have featured in films such as *Les Misérables*, *Snow White and the Huntsman* and *Jack the Giant Slayer*, and he's also a Royal Warrant holder, having supplied Prince Charles since the early 1980s.

If, like me, you love candles, this craft really will brighten the darkest winter day.

## YOU WILL NEED

Scissors · Sheet of paper · Ruler and pencil · Ready-made tapered candles in ivory · Appliqué wax sheets · Cutting mat and craft knife · Marker pen · White spirit · Lint-free cloth · Small paintbrush · Candle varnish

1 Cut a strip of paper (ours was about 4 cm wide) and wrap it around the widest part of one of the ready-made candles. Make a pencil mark where the paper overlaps.

2 Measure from the end of the paper to the pencil mark to discover the circumference of the candle, and therefore the length of the wax strips you need to cut.

3 Place a wax sheet on a cutting mat and use a craft knife and ruler to measure and cut it into strips of the desired width and length.

4 Using a permanent marker, make a small dot where the first strip is to be placed on the candle. Now mark where the other strips should go, spacing them equally to give a more professional finish.

5 Hold the first wax strip against the candle, covering the first dot you made, and press down until it sticks and the two ends meet. Rub the join gently with your thumb to help hide it. Repeat this step with the remaining wax strips.

6  Put a small amount of white spirit onto a corner of the lint-free cloth so that it is just damp. Wipe it very lightly over each stripe in one direction. This will remove any bits of dirt, fluff and fingerprints. Set aside to dry for 20 minutes.

7  Using a small paintbrush, carefully varnish over the wax strips, then stand the candle in a mug until the varnish is dry.

*It's best to do this craft in a warm room near a radiator. You want your candles to be warm so the wax will stick.*

*To make the appliqué wax sheets supple, warm them very, very slightly with a hairdryer. If you overheat them, they will melt.*

*For a sophisticated pre-Christmas drinks party, make these candles in black and ivory.*

# GOLD LEAF PEARS

If you really want to push the boat out this Christmas, edible gold leaf can turn pears into sensational place settings. Edible gold spray also works a treat, and is quite a bit cheaper.

## *YOU WILL NEED*

---

Edible gold leaf (1 sheet per pear) or edible gold spray  •  Egg wash (1 egg beaten with a little water), or sugar syrup (2 tbsp sugar boiled with 2 tbsp water for 5 minutes), if using gold leaf  •  Pastry brush  •  1 pear per place setting  •  Nice pen for writing names  •  Small luggage tags

1  If using gold leaf, it must be 'glued' to the fruit, so make an egg wash or sugar syrup and brush it over parts of a pear. (The fruit doesn't need to be completely covered with either glue or gold to get a great effect.)

2  Slide a sheet of gold leaf from the packet, but keep it attached to the paper. Begin tapping it onto the sticky parts of the pear to create a nice crackled effect. Repeat steps 1 and 2 to gild the rest of your pears.

3  If using edible gold spray, simply spray each pear until you're happy with the coverage and leave until touch-dry.

4  Write the name of each guest on a luggage tag in your best handwriting (if yours is terrible like mine, just ask someone else to do the writing – you don't want all that beauty spoilt by a messy scrawl).

5  Hang a luggage tag from the stem of each pear and put in the appropriate place.

# DIP-DYED PLACEMATS

Quilt-maker Polly Lyster developed her passion for cloth twenty years ago, when an indigo dyeing course fuelled her fascination for working with natural dyes and environmentally safe pigments. Her company, Dyeworks, produces the most beautiful range of natural colours dyed onto antique fabrics. Here she shares an idea for some gorgeous placemats dyed simply with onion skins and hot water. It's a great way of adding a bit of magic to old table linen.

## *YOU WILL NEED*

10-litre saucepan or galvanised bucket · 100 g onion skins · Wooden spoon · Colander · Large washing-up bowl · White or off-white linen placemats · Plastic bag (optional) · Hook or rack (optional)

1  Pour 6 litres of hot water into a saucepan and add the onion skins. Stir well, bring to the boil, then cover the pan with a lid and simmer for 15 minutes, stirring occasionally.

2  Strain through a colander into the washing-up bowl (you might need a second pair of hands to help you), then return the clear amber liquid to the original pan and place back on a low heat.

3  Fold a placemat in half lengthways and scrunch into even pleats along the fold.

4  Grasping the folded edge in one fist, immerse about 8 cm of the lower edges in the dye for 10 minutes. As this is quite a long time to be holding it by hand, you could suspend it if you prefer. Tie a plastic bag around the folded edge (the part you don't want to dye), leaving two long ends. Tie these ends to a hook or rack placed the appropriate distance above the dye.

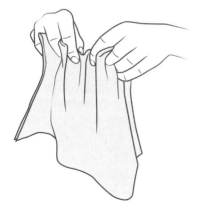

5  Lift the fabric from the dye, open it out and wash in warm water with mild soap. You can machine-wash the mats at a low temperature in non-biological detergent.

# CHAIR-BACK HERB BOUQUETS

While these herb bouquets look pretty on chair-backs and smell fantastic, they have another advantage: when they've dried up, you can use them to season your cooking. Waste not, want not.

Since medieval times people have been decorating their homes with herbs, believing they symbolised good luck. My bouquets contain bay for fame and fortune, rosemary for remembrance, sage for wisdom and lavender for devotion (also because I love the smell), so they couldn't be more perfect or decorative for chair-backs at Christmas-time. They're simply bound together with florist's tape, embellished with ribbon and then tied to the back of chairs.

## *YOU WILL NEED*

---

Selection of herbs, such as bay, rosemary, sage, lavender, thyme and marjoram • Scissors • Florist's tape • Ribbon

1 Group the herbs into attractive bunches and trim the stems to the same length.

2 Wrap florist's tape around the stems to keep them together, but not too tightly. Now wind ribbon around the tape and tie neatly, leaving two long ends (about 20 cm).

3 Using the long ends of the ribbon, tie the bouquets to the back of dining chairs so that the herbs hang downwards.

# CHRISTMAS FLORAL ARRANGEMENT

These delicate yet decadent table flowers by floral designer Kitten Grayson are a joy to recreate. Flower arranging is all about playing with colours and textures. Kitten doesn't tend to follow too many rules; instead she encourages people to go with their instincts about what looks pretty.

From experience, I'd say the best way to create a great display is to stand back and study your arrangement for balance after inserting every few stems. Also think about how it might look in the wild or in your back garden. I always fiddle to get it just the way I want it, but for me that's part of the pleasure and relaxation of arranging flowers. Only plumping cushions is on a par.

## YOU WILL NEED

Scissors  ·  2–3 stems of hypericum berries per vase  ·  Clear glass or crystal vases about 10–15 cm tall  ·  3 or 5 roses per vase (odd numbers look best; we used a mixture of red piano roses and black bacarra roses)  ·  3–5 hellebore stems per vase  ·  A few extra flowers to fill any gaps

1 Cut the berry stems 2–3 cm taller than your vase and pop them in.

2 Cut the stems of 2 or 3 red roses at an angle and a little shorter than the berries. (The number depends on how many bacarra roses you plan to add: with 2 red roses use 1 black rose, and with 3 red roses use 2 black roses, so the total number is always odd.) Remove the leaves and thorns so the stems look neat. Remember, they will be visible through the glass.

3 Place a stem of hellebore in the centre, making it taller than the rest. The overall shape of the arrangement is equivalent to a castle with a central tower, so think of this hellebore as your tower flower. Continue adding the hellebores,

criss-crossing them with the other stems so they all support one another. Don't overcrowd things: just like people, flowers need to breathe.

4 Add the bacarra rose(s) where you feel it (or they) work best. When you stand back to assess the arrangement, you're looking for balance and a sense of stability. Turn the vase around so you can check that it has these qualities if it will be viewed from all sides. If it will sit against a wall, you only need to focus on the front, as the back won't be visible.

5 Look for gaps that need filling, and continue adding hellebores until you're happy with the arrangement.

# THE PERFECT CHRISTMAS ARRANGEMENTS

- Bold flowerheads, like those of roses, work beautifully in small arrangements, while hellebores provide movement and berries give texture. For summer arrangements I'm a huge fan of sweet peas and hydrangeas. Remember that dried hydrangeas are ideal later in the year for winter displays.

- Carnations are a cheap alternative to roses, but I recommend buying them from a florist rather than a supermarket because they tend to have much fuller heads. Also, buying from a local florist makes a real difference to the flower market industry in this country.

- Always ask your florist when the flowers came in. That way you'll know how fresh they are and how long they might last. Most freshly cut flowers will last up to seven days, but there are no guarantees.

- Leave making the arrangement for your Christmas table to the last possible minute as central heating will make the flowers go limp. If you must buy them a while in advance, store them in a cool place, such as a garage, to prolong freshness.

# CHRISTMAS CRACKERS

A British man called Tom Smith invented crackers in the 1840s, and now they're an essential part of our Christmas festivities. Literally millions are pulled every year, and there's nothing worse than a cracker that doesn't pull with a bang. That's what Clare Hutchison of Froufrou & Thomas said to me several years ago when we made crackers together at Meadowgate. They were the best crackers ever, handmade with specially chosen gifts inside.

Since then, I've picked my own presents to fill my crackers. It's more personal and it's way more fun. You can tailor them to your guests and really have a laugh with the things you put inside. Remember, you can buy paper hats online and handwrite your own jokes or riddles as well. The children love doing this.

Clare's main piece of advice is to use luxurious papers – it's what makes her crackers so lovely. She also embellishes them with baubles, beads and beautiful ribbons to ensure each one is a little work of art on the table.

# *YOU WILL NEED*

---

Good-quality Christmas wrapping paper · Ruler and pencil ·
Scissors · Cracker snaps · Glue gun or water-based glue · 3 empty toilet
rolls, or 1 empty kitchen paper roll cut into 3 equal pieces (1 roll
stays in the cracker, the others are removed after shaping) · Ribbon · Little
gifts · Embellishments, such as beads, baubles, berries or leaves

1  Take a piece of wrapping paper, mark out a rectangle 33 × 20 cm, then cut it out. Fold in 10 cm along each short edge, then snip out small triangles no more than 1 cm deep along the folds. About 8–10 triangles is ideal.

2  Now it's on to the cracker snap. (In case you're wondering how these work, the two sides of the snap are coated with a tiny bit of gunpowder and when they're pulled apart, the friction ignites the bang.) Open out the paper, wrong side up. Put a dab of glue at each end of the snap and stick it parallel to one long side of the paper, about 2 cm in from the edge.

3  Place your 3 toilet roll tubes on the paper, as shown. Roll the paper around the tubes and up towards the snap. Put a thin line of glue along the very top edge of the paper and quickly roll the final bit to stick the seam down. If using a glue gun, it will dry straight away. If using water-based glue, give it a minute or so to dry.

4  Tie a ribbon fairly tightly between two of the tubes in the cracker. Insert a gift, joke and hat in the opposite end, then tie a ribbon between the other two tubes. Now remove the end tubes.

5  Using dabs of glue, decorate your cracker with your chosen embellishments. Basically, anything goes. For instance, you can colour-theme your crackers in gold or silver, or opt for a wonderful mix of Christmas colours.

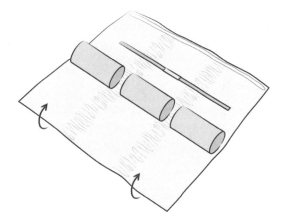

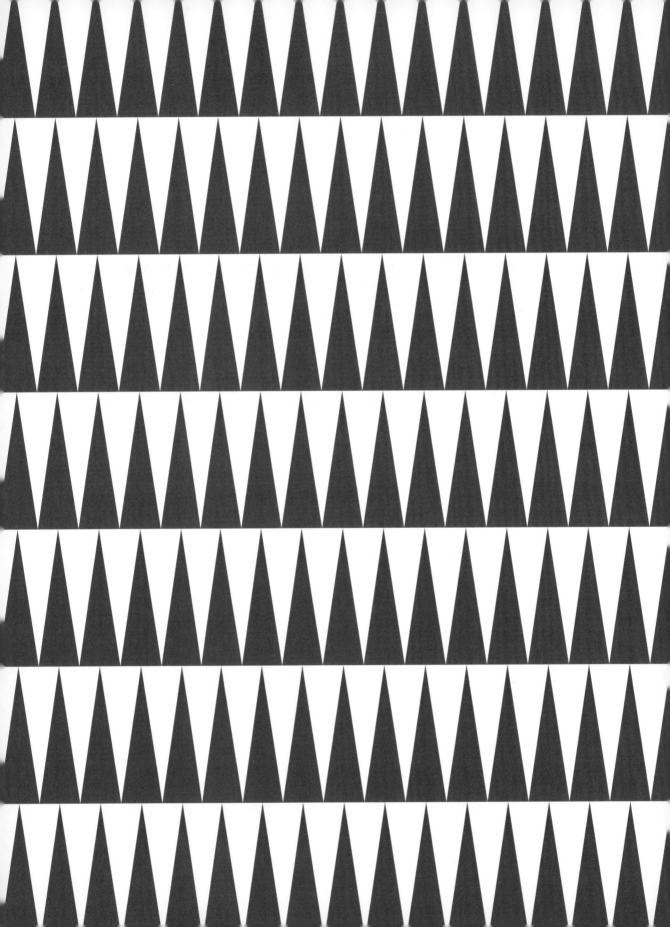

# PERFECT PRESENTS

—

*IT REALLY IS THE THOUGHT THAT COUNTS*

I pull out all the stops at Christmas as far as presents are concerned. I think it's because I struggle to remember birthdays, so at Christmas I have a blow-out. I have a large family and *ten* godchildren, so my present list is always huge. Last year it contained seventy-three different people.

For very close family and friends I put together quite a specific buying list, which I think about and add to throughout the year. Even at the height of summer, if I see something that reminds me specifically of someone, I will buy it and set it aside for Christmas. My other half, Ben, is an all-year-round gift-giver. I'm constantly urging him to save the things he buys for me and the boys for Christmas (or a birthday/anniversary), but he can't. Immediacy is his thing. Not one to knock a gift in the face, I can live with that.

For everyone else I usually try to create a theme, otherwise I'd go stark, staring mad trying to think of different gifts. Last year I did scarves; the year before it was ceramic bowls by one of my favourite companies, Brixton Pottery, and the year before that it was bracelets. I also did magazine subscriptions one year, which everyone loved.

I start the bulk of my present-buying during the autumn half-term holiday, a habit I acquired from my mother. When I was young, she always took me to London during that time and bought most of her Christmas presents. She takes gift-buying very seriously, and she still spends a lot of time seeking out the right present for everyone.

I believe the world divides over the way we buy presents: people either plan, make and buy well in advance, or leave it late and chuck money at it. Some of my most successful gifts have been second-hand finds, partly luck of course, but that comes from my mantra of always keeping an eye out for presents no matter what time of year it is. That said, the gifts I buy a long time in advance of Christmas always run the risk of getting forgotten and being rediscovered in February when the party is long over, so keep a list of what you've bought.

In Victorian times, when Christmas became the principal celebration of the year, gift-giving was modest. Things such as food, dried fruit, nuts and handmade goodies were hung on the tree rather than placed beneath it. I love these traditions, so I'm spreading the word that it's fashionable to give handmade presents again.

In an ideal world we'd *make* all the presents we want to give, but that's never going to happen. Luckily, there are more and more people out there making handmade, unique and unusual wares at affordable prices. Websites such as www.notonthehighstreet.com have made the task of finding personal presents for loved ones a joy. Last year I bought a handmade embroidered bag for a teacher at my son's school, with her name on it. She absolutely loved it, as do the children. See the useful addresses at the end of this book, or search online for people making wonderful things right here in Britain. I also have a lot of success at Christmas Craft Fairs. Last Christmas I found some lovely cushions for my mum and sister, and a brilliant waistcoat made from old Indian fabrics for my father-in-law. It's well worth doing the rounds at your local fairs.

On *Kirstie's Vintage Christmas* show Iman Ahmed and I made a sledge with James Harvey (www.jamesharveyfurniture.com) for his children Heather and little Olympia. I have to say it was one of the loveliest, most fun things I've ever made, and such a special present for their family. If you're thinking of a special gift for someone, definitely consider a craft course. Woodwork is brilliant because it's a skill that can be developed. Also, the things you make, like Iman's sledge, can become family heirlooms that pass down the generations.

One of the best gifts I ever received was a DVD of the film *Footloose*, one of my favourite movies when I was younger. It wasn't expensive or vintage or handmade, but it was beautifully wrapped and reminded me of a carefree time in my life. I watched it immediately and have watched it many times since.

When I'm buying for my numerous godchildren, I simply head for a big toyshop because children want what all their friends have, and that tends to

involve plastic and what they've seen on TV. I go with a long list and nail it in one day in October, before the rush and fights begin, then I get these gifts wrapped and delivered just as soon as possible so that the job is done. Although I go to one of the big stores, I also shop at our local Honiton Toyshop because it's such a lovely, traditional place, and I think it's important to support and sustain it. The toys they sell are individual, and although a little more expensive, they're worth it. These are the toys the boys have had since they were born and that I'll keep for my grandchildren.

Good luck with your present-buying. It's definitely the thought that counts.

These are some of my favourite websites if you're struggling for original gift ideas and don't have time to make them:

- www.notonthehighstreet.com

- www.baileys.co.uk

- www.labourandwait.co.uk

- www.yolke.co.uk

- www.sirplus.co.uk

- www.frombritainwithlove.co.uk

- www.pedlars.co.uk

- www.re-foundobjects.com

# KIRSTIE'S THRIFTY & THOUGHTFUL GIFT IDEAS

Anything handmade. Obviously anything you make yourself will go down a storm, and this chapter is full of brilliant projects.

Second-hand books. These are always a winner, particularly on subjects that feed passions, such as cooking or interiors. For more ideas on how to personalise books, there's a brilliant stamp project on page 128.

Old photographs. I was recently sent a 1991 picture of my best friend and me with Bobby Robson in Bangalore, India. It's a brilliant image that will look lovely in an old frame, of which I have many. For someone special, try blowing up photographs as well.

Sweets. Last year the boys were given a basket of their favourite sweets all wrapped in cellophane; it also included a mug with their picture on. As they could see everything in the basket, they got thoroughly excited and prodded it in anticipation all the way up to Christmas. Even jelly beans in a jam jar are brilliant with a bit of personalising.

Pretty teacups or mugs. I buy a lot of royal mugs because they're fun and colourful.

Photographs of children. All parents love receiving photographs of their children.

Bowls and jugs. Basically all ceramics, new or second-hand, work a treat for me. Try starting a collection for someone that you can add to in future. Brixton Pottery or Cornish Ware are good for this, or go with a theme they already have.

Rainbows. I love anything rainbow-like, such as a rainbow of socks or pants or even ties, especially in a nice box prettily labelled and ribboned.

DVDs. Everyone has favourite films that they love watching time and again. It doesn't take a lot of digging to find out what your friends' old favourites are.

Mix CDs. Every year we receive a Christmas mix CD from our neighbour, and we play it right through Christmas. This is an old-school, handmade present that never fails to please.

Beauty hamper. For my girlfriends, I love putting together a selection of my favourite products, such as lip gloss and hand cream. For a handmade treat, try the bath bombes on page 12.

Sales. It's a real bonus to find future presents in the sales and stow them away.

Scarves and fingerless gloves. Everyone needs them and if, like me, you've got lots of people to give to, you can buy in bulk.

Old postcards or telegrams. See the one I was given on page 000.

Family memorabilia. Old family photos or heirlooms make great gifts if dusted off. A few years ago my other half borrowed an original scrapbook made for his brother by his grandmother in the 1970s. He had each page copied and bound, and gave one to every member of his family. They were all thrilled.

Charitable donations. These are good for those who have a cause dear to their hearts, such as my Snowflake Appeal on page 244.

# LAVENDER BATH CREAMERS

One of my favourite gifts to give friends is a 'beauty basket' full of the products I love. This recipe for bath creamers from designer Jenny Elesmore makes a perfect addition, and can be made alongside the bath bombes on page 112. Arrange them in a basket or box, or simply wrap them in cellophane and tie with ribbon. Attach a handwritten label stating the ingredients you've used to inspire your recipient.

## YOU WILL NEED

100 g cocoa butter • Plastic jug • 50 g shea butter • 50 ml almond oil • 2–4 ml lavender essential oil • Small paper cases for moulds • Rosebuds

1  Put the cocoa butter in a plastic jug and microwave on High for about 20 seconds, until the butter has melted.

2  Add the shea butter to the jug and microwave again until that has melted too.

3  Stir in the almond oil and lavender essential oil, then allow to cool for a few minutes.

4  Arrange the paper cases on a tray. Spoon the mixture into the cases and leave to become cloudy and cool (about 10 minutes).

5  Once the creamers are cloudy, insert a rosebud into the centre of each one. Set aside for 24 hours, and the creamers are then ready to use in a warm bath.

# LAVENDER BATH BOMBES

This recipe for bath bombes by Jenny Elesmore is just brilliant. Lavender is my scent of choice, but if it's not your cup of tea, you can change the fragrance by choosing different essential oils, such as rose, geranium or marigold, and add matching flower buds or petals. If you're making the bombes as a present, they go fantastically well with the bath creamers on page 111. This recipe makes about four.

## *YOU WILL NEED*

---

450 g bicarbonate of soda  •  300 g citric acid granules  •  150 g cornflour  •  2½ tsp lavender essential oil in a spray bottle  •  4 large bombe moulds that divide in half  •  Sunflower oil  •  Pinch of lavender buds  •  Bulldog clips

**All the equipment for this project can be bought online from any soap-making website.**

1  Sift the bicarbonate of soda, citric acid and cornflour into a large bowl, then mix well.

2  Gently spray two shots of the lavender oil thinly and evenly onto the flour mixture and stir together. (The mixture will bubble and swell, so proceed with caution.) Repeat this step carefully until the mixture just about holds together like wet sand when pressed firmly between your fingers. (This needs less oil than you think.)

3  Grease your bombe moulds lightly with sunflower oil, place some lavender buds in each one, then pack the oil mixture firmly into both halves. Press together and fasten with a bulldog clip. Leave the bombes overnight to harden.

4  The following day, open the moulds and use a twisting action to remove the bombes; they should be firmly set in a ball shape. Leave them for another day to dry completely, then they are ready to use.

# SCREEN-PRINTED TOY PANDA

The art of screen-printing has its origins in Japanese stencilling, but the method known today is thought to have come from Manchester at the turn of the twentieth century and was a process used by the designer William Morris.

To get started you'll need a screen, which you can make yourself by stapling mesh evenly and taut over a cheap canvas stretcher frame, and a squeegee that fits inside it. Alternatively, you can buy a kit for around £30. The equipment can be used again and again to print your own designs onto t-shirts, cushions, curtains, tablecloths, bags or whatever you like, so it's a good investment.

This toy panda project by textile designer Zeena Shah is a very cool Christmas gift to kick off your screen-printing prowess. It's perfect for a child, or a sweet gift for a friend – a little bit of monochrome magic. The finished toy measures 24 × 15 cm.

## YOUWILLNEED

---

Tracing paper and hard pencil  •  Cutting mat and craft knife  •  30 × 20 cm piece of natural fabric, such as cotton, calico or linen  •  Silk screen  • Masking tape  •  Black heat-setting fabric ink  •  Squeegee  •  Hairdryer  • 30 × 20 cm piece of backing fabric, such as a piece of old sheet or curtain  •  Scissors  •  Pins  •  Sewing machine and suitable thread  •  Polyester toy stuffing

1  Trace around the panda template on page 232, then place it on a cutting mat and cut around it. Now cut out all the shaded areas, as these are the parts that will print.

2  Place the stencil on your chosen fabric. Sit the screen over the stencil with the mesh side uppermost and make a masking tape box 2.5 cm bigger all round than the stencil. Overlap the tape at the corners to make sure there are no gaps through which ink might accidentally leak.

Turn the screen over, mesh side down, and position the masked box over the stencil, checking once again that there are no gaps.

3  Spoon a line of ink onto the strip of masking tape above the stencil. Position your squeegee just above it, then, holding the screen firmly with one hand, pull the squeegee down towards you at a 45-degree angle to spread the ink across the frame and through the cut-out parts of the stencil. Firm pressure is the key to getting a

crisp print all over (see Tips). Pull the ink across again, making sure that all areas of the stencil are evenly covered.

6 Place the backing fabric and stencilled fabric right sides together. Draw around the panda shape about 2.5 cm from its edge, then cut around the line to create a nice border.

4 Lift off the screen and peel off the stencil, which will have stuck to it. Throw the stencil away, then wash the ink off the screen with cold water as soon as possible. It's vital to prevent ink drying into the screen and blocking the mesh. Set aside to dry naturally.

5 Use a hairdryer to dry your print, then press with a medium-hot iron for a minute or so (or according to the packet instructions on the ink) to heat-set the colour; this is what makes the fabric washable.

7 Pin the fabric together and machine around it about 2.5 cm from the edge, leaving a 10 cm gap on one side through which the polyester stuffing can be inserted.

8 Cut triangular notches in any inward curves, then turn the fabric right side out and press firmly with an iron.

9 Push the stuffing into the gap until the toy is nicely padded, then slipstitch the gap closed.

---

*Paper stencils have to be thrown away after one use, so if you want to do lots of the same print, make several stencils at once.*

*It's advisable to do a test print on newspaper or a scrap of cloth before printing on your fabric.*

*It's important to hold the frame firmly while pulling the squeegee to avoid a blurred print. If you find it difficult, ask a friend to help. Alternatively, fix the screen in place with a G-clamp or weight it down.*

---

# FAMILY SCRAPBOOK

Scrapbooks are lovely gifts. They're all about preserving a bit of history that's personal to whoever you're giving it to. They can contain anything that provokes a memory, from photographs and ticket stubs to cards, invitations and scraps of fabric. I always think it's good to make a scrapbook that can be added to, so definitely include some blank pages at the back.

The instructions below describe a professional yet simple method of hand binding, which involves reinforcing the spine edge of each page with a strip of card. This makes the finished book much more durable. When it comes to punching holes in them, you'll need to be meticulous and patient to make sure they all match up. But don't worry if they don't completely align. There's beauty in imperfection too.

## YOU WILL NEED

Patterned, heavyweight paper (we used hand-blocked A0 sheets from Paperchase, which we cut down to A4) · Ruler and pencil · Family photographs · Spray adhesive (this allows items to be repositioned) or decorative photo corners · Embellishments, such as stickers, tags, découpaged pictures, collage, glitter, buttons, ribbons and coloured craft tape · Pretty labels or tags · Card, for reinforcing the spine edge · Scalpel and/or scissors · Small Dremel drill or sturdy hole punch · Ribbon, yarn, string or twine, for binding · Nice pen

1 Take each sheet of paper and draw a faint line 1 cm down one side that will form the spine edge. This is the binding allowance.

2 Arrange your photographs on the sheets in a visually interesting order that tells a story without words.

3 Once you're happy with the arrangement, use a little spray adhesive on each corner of the photos to stick them in place. If, like me, you are obsessed with detail, you can find really beautiful photo corners online. The best ones always seem to come from the USA.

4 You can now embellish the pages with anything you like, such as stickers, tags and collage.

5 Decide which is going to be the binding edge of your scrapbook. Now you must cut strips of card to help reinforce that edge on each page. The card can be thick or thin, depending how chunky you want the spine to be. Make it the same length as your pages and about 1 cm wide.

6 Glue a reinforcing strip to each page and allow to dry. When it comes to reinforcing the cover, remember to glue the strip on the underside so that it doesn't show.

7  Now it's time to make holes along the binding edge. The size of them depends on the width of the ribbon or yarn being used to bind the album. In our case it was 3–4 mm wide, so we made five equally spaced holes about 5 mm wide and 5 mm in from the edge. Mark them out carefully with a ruler and pencil, then cut them using either a small Dremel drill with the correctly sized drill bit, or use a sturdy hole punch. Alternatively, get a local print shop to do it for you (it won't cost much). While you're there, you can, if you wish, get them to neatly guillotine the pages, and to make multiple colour copies, which you can also bind and give as presents.

8  Put the pages together in the correct order, then follow the diagram below to thread your ribbon through the holes. This is important so that the binding works correctly and evenly across the spine edge.

9  Once both ends of the ribbon are through the central hole, gently pull both ends away from each other to tighten the bind, then tie the ribbon into a bow. The binding will look like this from the back.

10  Stick a pretty decoration label or tag on the front, maybe embellished with a nicely handwritten title or message.

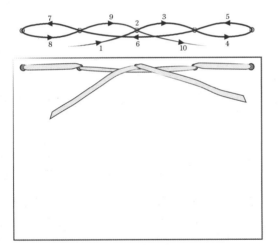

A MERRY CHRISTMAS TO YOU

# BEJEWELLED CHRISTMAS TREE

I first discovered these beautiful trees at a garage sale in New York. Since then, I've been longing to recreate them myself. It was designer and illustrator Poppy Chancellor who went to town making this one. It's the best craft if, like me, you have years worth of abandoned costume jewellery that you'd like to turn into something spectacular. While I was looking into the history of costume jewellery Christmas trees, I came across a brilliant blog by Cathy of California. She has a copy of *Classic Jewelled Treasures* by Bobi Hall from 1973; bejewelled objects were definitely a big deal on the US crafts circuit back then, but I don't think they ever made it to Britain . . . until now.

## YOU WILL NEED

Old or new picture frame with wooden backing board, glass removed (ours is about A3 size) · Tape measure · Piece of fabric to cover the backing board (we used felt) · Scissors · Strong spray adhesive · Trimmings, such as ribbon or braid · Selection of costume jewellery · Needle-nose pliers or jewellery wire cutters · Metal file or medium sandpaper · Lidded plastic container · Glue gun (this is essential)

1  Remove the backing board from the frame, measure it, then cut a piece of fabric about 5 cm bigger all round. Using spray adhesive, glue the fabric to the board and allow to dry before returning it to the frame.

2  Use trimmings to create an outline of a Christmas tree, its bucket and star.

3  Think about how your blings might be used. It's good to keep some things whole: a pearl necklace or diamanté bracelet, for example, can be used to snake across your design and act as tinsel. We carefully cut my long pearl necklace into sections and tied off the ends to make shorter strands. For brooches and suchlike, gently remove the soldered backs using the pliers and wire cutters. If any stones come loose, simply glue them back in. Using the file or sandpaper, sand any rough edges so the jewels sit evenly on the fabric. Put all the bits in your plastic container.

4  Now start putting your jewels inside the outline. I'm a fan of symmetry and also very neat, so I paid a lot of attention to balancing each side. Trust me, you'll fiddle a *lot*.

5  When you're satisfied, stick the jewels down with a glue gun. Allow to dry for 24 hours and, hey presto – a beautiful gift that's sure to become a cherished heirloom.

# REINVENTING OLD CASHMERE

Clothes designer Christa Davis has been reworking and upcycling cashmere for more than twenty years, and she firmly believes that a loyal, much-cherished cashmere garment is more than a piece of clothing – it's part of your history. Christa runs a surgery where people send their jumpers and cardigans for repair, and she's shared a few of her clever cures with me. They'll transform your well-worn pieces into brilliant Christmas gifts, guaranteed.

---

## SNUG FOR A PUG

A snug dog coat is a great thing to make with a shrunken jumper. And don't worry if you don't know anyone with a pug. Simply alter the length of the coat pattern to suit the back of your chosen pooch.

**YOU WILL NEED**
- 1 shrunken jumper (the bigger the dog, the bigger the jumper you'll need)
- 4–6 metres cotton or satin bias binding
- Scissors
- Pins
- Sewing machine and suitable thread
- Hand-sewing needle
- 4 vintage or wooden buttons

1  Shrink the jumper again by washing it on a 60°C machine cycle (90°C will overfelt it). Dry flat, then steam iron.

2  Cut off the arms, neck and bottom rib of the jumper, then cut up the side seams so you have two pieces – a front and a back.

3  Take your dog's measurements, as indicated below. Copy the pattern pieces on page 233 to the size of your dog, then cut them out.

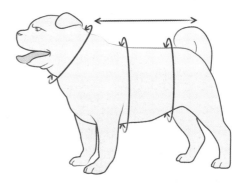

4  Lay pattern A on the front piece of the jumper and cut around the shape. Lay patterns B and C on the back part of the jumper and cut around them too.

5  Open out the bias binding and pin it around pattern C (the collar), leaving a gap of about 10 cm in the middle of the straight side, where it will be attached to the coat. Using a straight stitch, machine around the crease in the binding. Fold the binding over to the other side and machine around it about 3 mm from the edge so all the layers are stitched together.

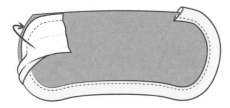

6  Stitch binding all the way around pattern B (the underbelly) in the same way as in step 5.

7  Pin a length of binding along the centre of pattern A (the back) and machine it along both edges.

8  Pin the collar to the narrowest end of pattern A, then pin and machine bias binding all around the raw edges as in step 5.

9  Sew the buttons and buttonholes into position, then pop the snug on the pug.

## ROSE PIN

When there's no hope for prolonging the life of a jumper or cardigan, you can use it to make this lovely accessory. Upcycling and repurposing is something I've always been passionate about.

YOU WILL NEED
- Old jumper
- Scissors
- Needle
- Thread that matches the jumper
- Child-friendly safety pin

1  Cut the bottom rib off the jumper, then trim the cut edge to make the rib 5 cm wide and 36 cm long. Set the excess aside.

2  Using a needle and double thread, sew a line of running stitch 1 cm in from the raw edge of the rib. Pull the thread so the rib bunches up as much as possible.

3 Start rolling the gathered rib round and around so that it forms a rose shape. Check and adjust the shape before tightly winding the thread around the bottom of it and making a few stitches to hold it together. Cut the thread.

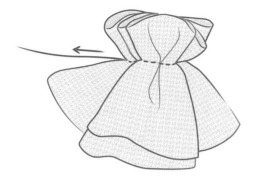

4 Cut a 4 cm circle from the excess rib and place it on the base of the rose. Sew it in place with small running stitches, making tucks as you sew and gradually concealing the base until it forms a ball shape.

5 Sew the safety pin onto the base of the rose and it's ready to wear.

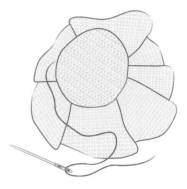

# PATCHING

Here's the perfect medicine for a cashmere elbow or underarm that's given up the ghost. Patch it using colourful patterned fabric scraps cut into ovals, stars or triangles, or even non-symmetrical shapes. The great thing is that you're saving a woolly from the scrap pile and creating a stylish new piece of clothing.

YOU WILL NEED
- Pencil and thin cardboard
- Scissors
- Scraps of soft fabric, such as cashmere, silk or cotton
- Tailor's chalk
- Worn-out jumper or cardigan
- Pins
- Sewing machine and suitable thread

1  Decide what shape you'd like your patches to be and sketch it onto the cardboard. It should be large enough to cover the holes in the jumper. Cut out the template, then place on your scrap fabric. Chalk around it twice, then cut out.

2  Turn the jumper inside out, then fold the arms flat as shown below to reveal the elbow holes. Make sure the arms are folded equally and extend the same distance below the hem of the jumper so the patches can be placed symmetrically on each elbow.

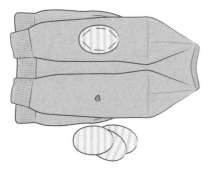

3  Pin the patches into position, right side down, and machine them to the sleeves using a small zigzag stitch around the edge. When done, repeat with a second row 1.25 cm in from the first.

4  If you're patching an underarm, fold the fabric patch into quarters to find the centre of it, then position that point under the arm where all the seams meet. Pin into place, keeping each quarter in the right position. Machine two zigzag rows  as in step 3.

5  Turn the jumper right side out and cut away the holey cashmere just inside the inner line of zigzag to reveal the patch below. Press with a steam iron before wearing.

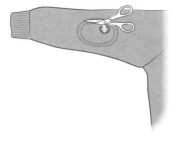

*This patching process can be applied to all sorts of jumpers suffering from unsightly stains or moth holes. It can also be used to jazz up tired old woollies with cotton shoulder patches.*

*At the first sign of moth damage in your cashmere or other woollies, put them in the freezer for one week to kill any moth larvae, then wash in warm water (40°C), dry flat and steam iron. Check at regular intervals and repeat the same treatment as necessary.*

# STAMP CRAFTS

I've been obsessed with stamping things since I was a little girl. With a bit of imagination, there are so many things you can create with stamps you've made yourself, bought or had custom-made from your own designs, including cushion covers, t-shirts and drawstring travel bags.

One of the best things about lino-cut stamps is the natural inconsistency between each print made with them. It means that each is unique and clearly handmade – a world away from mass-production.

---

## LINO-STAMPED HAND TOWELS

Textile designer Zeena Shah specialises in making beautiful home accessories, and offers beginners' classes in making lino-cut stamps. Her design for hand-printed towels is a lovely idea, especially for a gift. Wrap them simply in brown paper and ribbon, and use your stamp to make a matching card or gift tag.

YOU WILL NEED
- Pencil and paper
- Scissors
- Piece of linoleum (speed carve lino is easier to cut than real lino)
- Lino cutter
- Cutting board
- Ink pad
- 100% cotton towels
- Fabric paint (washable)
- Small paint tray
- 2 rollers

1  To make a lino-cut stamp, you need a template, so draw a design onto paper. It's best to start with something simple and large that won't be too complex to cut out. Remember, it will appear as a mirror image on the fabric, so draw your design in reverse, especially if working with letters.

2  Cut out the template, place it on the lino and draw around it. Using a lino cutter, gouge away the surface surrounding the outline. The idea is to leave the shape standing proud so only that part will print. It's a good idea to warm the lino on a radiator to make it easier to cut out, especially in winter.

3  When you have finished carving, test the stamp by pressing it on an ink pad and then onto paper. If the stamp picks up any ink where you don't want it, just keep carving until you are happy with the test print. Clean the ink off the lino with a damp cloth.

4  Spread out a towel in readiness for the printing process, then pour your fabric paint into the tray. Roll a roller in it, and then run the roller over the stamp, making sure the paint is evenly distributed.

# PERSONALISED STATIONERY

There are some amazing machine-cut stamps available in shops and online. Some firms (such as the English Stamp Company) offer a bespoke service making stamps from your own artwork. These are great gifts in themselves, and brilliant for creating a range of customised stationery.

**YOU WILL NEED**
- Machine-cut stamp(s)
- Ink pads in various colours
- Scrap paper, for test prints
- Blank stationery, such as cards, envelopes or notebooks, in a natural colour

5 Gently press the stamp onto the towel, then roll over it with a dry roller to thoroughly press in the paint. Carefully lift off the stamp, then repeat the paint and rolling process until you've achieved the design you want. Leave to dry according to the paint manufacturer's instructions, ideally overnight.

6 To seal the design onto the towel, iron it with a dry iron. Remember, fabric paints are water-based, so if you go over the print with a steam iron, all your hard work will be ruined. It's a good idea to wash your towel to soften the paint before giving the towel away. Do this according to the fabric paint instructions.

1 Cover your work surface with old newspaper to protect it. Lay your stamp on its back and firmly press an ink pad onto it. If it's quite a big stamp, move the inkpad to other areas to make sure it's completely covered.

2 To make a test print, take a scrap piece of paper and press the stamp down firmly for several seconds with the palms of your hands. Examine the print to see if the ink is too light or if you're applying more pressure to one area than another. Continue doing test prints until you're happy with the result, then move on to stamping the real thing.

*Always clean your stamps after use or if you're changing colours.*

*I'm a big fan of stamping books, new or old, when giving them as gifts. You can stamp a message, image or name inside, or even along the cut edge of the pages.*

*As an alternative to carving stamps from lino, try carving pencil erasers. It's easy to create delicate flower motifs or cool geometric shapes.*

# EDIBLE GIFTS

---

## THE TASTIEST
## PRESENTS OF ALL

I've heard that the Duchess of Cambridge made Her Majesty the Queen a hamper for Christmas. What an inspired and personal thing to give to the woman who has everything. I'm sure she was absolutely thrilled with it – who wouldn't be? Edible gifts make brilliant Christmas presents because they're not just delicious, they show you've put in thought and effort too.

Hampers are notoriously expensive to buy at Christmas, but creating your own contents and buying a basket to hold everything can save you a fortune, especially if you're making more than one hamper. You can make batches of biscuits (see page 215), or jars of Victoria's chutney (see page 138) or Susan's hot cranberry sauce (see page 140), thus creating several gifts at once. And the bonus of making edible gifts is that any surplus can be consumed at home. In fact, make it a rule. There must be surplus.

My grandparents used to give my mum and dad a whole smoked salmon every year, and my fellow TV presenter, Phil Spencer, always gives me a ham from Farmer Guy (see page 164). It arrives in a traditional wooden crate and we always look forward to it. Last year my other half received a hamper from his

colleagues, and each thing inside was made by a different person. It included chutney, sloe gin, homemade harissa and horseradish; I don't think he's ever been happier with a Christmas gift. There's something about food gifts that people just love.

This chapter is full of edible gift ideas that would make fantastic individual foodie presents, such as the spice blends on page 151 and Big Ridge's chocolate mendiants on page 154. For more impact, make them part of a cracking hamper. There are even a few foodie ideas that the kids will love. Try the gingerbread house on page 142 and the passion fruit marshmallows on page 159 – these are so yummy that they don't last more than five minutes in my house.

With these things in mind, start saving your empty jars and look out for cheap and second-hand baskets that you can embellish. Book a couple of days in the diary and crank up the Christmas tunes because cooking your presents to the sound of carols can be a whole lot nicer than fighting over parking spaces and spending hours in high street queues. Before you know it, you'll have a brilliant stash of delicious edible goodies ready to go.

# BOXING DAY CHUTNEY

What Victoria Cranfield doesn't know about chutneys, jellies and jams quite simply isn't worth knowing. She's won countless medals for her preserves, including a double gold in the World's Marmalade Awards. Victoria is one of my heroines, as not only did she help me to make a delicious damson jam to serve as part of my prize-winning afternoon tea, but a few Christmases ago we made this chutney to add to a hamper for my dad.

Chutney is basically a sweet and sour condiment made with fruits, sugar and vinegar. It's often made weeks, sometimes even months, in advance to give the ingredients time to mix and mature. However, Victoria's recipe is edible straight away, which is great if you need to cook up a last-minute gift. It will make about five 200 g jars, and it goes brilliantly with Christmas Day leftovers.

## YOU WILL NEED

---

1 kg naturally dried apricots, chopped (these are brown and taste far better than the orange type) • 175 g dates, pitted and chopped • 450 g raisins • Juice of 8 oranges (about 600 ml) • 900 g onions sliced • 900 g cooking apples, chopped • 340 g cranberries • 1.2 litres cider vinegar • 50 g fresh root ginger, peeled and finely diced • 1 tbsp coarse sea salt • 1 tsp mixed spice • Zest of 2 oranges • 1 kg white sugar

1  First sterilise your jam jars. Preheat the oven to its lowest setting, then place the jars and lids in it upside down for 30 minutes.

2  Place the dried fruit in a bowl, add the orange juice and stir well. Set aside to marinate for 20 minutes, by which time the mixture should have absorbed all the juice.

3  Meanwhile, place everything except the sugar in a saucepan and bring gently to the boil. The aim is for the onions to become transparent, the apple to break down and the cranberries to start popping, so simmer for just 5 minutes, stirring occasionally, to retain some texture.

4  Add the marinated fruit to the saucepan with the sugar. Mix well and bring back to the boil, stirring constantly or the contents will catch and taint the chutney. The free liquid will start to thicken quite quickly and the chutney can then be jarred.

5  Carefully ladle the mixture into the sterilised jars, filling them as near to the top as possible. Seal tightly, then label and date.

# HOT CRANBERRY SAUCE

Just over two years ago Susan McCann began selling her delicious homemade strawberry and chilli condiment at farmers' markets and delis around Scotland. She called her special recipe SIMPLYaddCHILLI because that's pretty much what you do with it – add it to everything you eat and cook. I love Susan's chilli strawberry pots so much that I asked her to do something Christmassy for this book. She came up with a brilliant twist on cranberry sauce.

For me, there's nothing better than hearing success stories from people who've taken a risk to go it alone. Susan, like so many others in this book, is an inspiration for anyone thinking of taking a leap into the unknown for something they truly believe in.

This hot cranberry sauce is a great addition to a hamper, and it will take your turkey and chicken to a whole new level. The recipe makes about five 200 g jars (remember to sterilise them, see page 138).

## *YOU WILL NEED*

---

460 g cranberries, fresh or frozen • 300 g red peppers, deseeded and roughly chopped • 2 whole habañero chillies • 3 garlic cloves, peeled • Juice of 1 lemon • 60 ml cider vinegar • 100 g jam sugar • 300 g granulated sugar

1  Put the cranberries, peppers, chillies, garlic cloves and lemon juice into a blender. With the motor running, slowly add the vinegar until you have a thick consistency.

2  Put both lots of sugar into a large saucepan. Pour in the cranberry mixture and stir well. Bring to the boil slowly, then cook at a rolling boil for about 5 minutes, skimming off any foam that rises to the top.

3  Pot up into sterilised jars, seal tightly, then label and date. Enjoy straight away with turkey, chicken or cheese, or store in a cool, dry place for up to three months. Once open, keep refrigerated.

# GINGERBREAD HOUSE

Gingerbread houses are serious fantasy food for children. Scrap that – they're everyone's fantasy food. They've become a pretty chic thing to make in recent years, but I have to admit I found constructing a property from sugar and gingerbread quite a challenge when all I really wanted to do was eat it.

This is a brilliant recipe for building your house from scratch by food writer Louisa Carter. You can embellish it with your favourite sweets and watch eyes light up when the lucky person discovers it's for them.

## *YOU WILL NEED*

---

Pencil, tracing paper and card · Scissors

### FOR THE GINGERBREAD

250 g butter · 200 g dark muscovado sugar · 100 ml golden syrup · 650 g plain flour · 2 tsp bicarbonate of soda · 2 tbsp ground ginger

### FOR THE ROYAL ICING

1 large egg white · 300 g icing sugar · Few drops of lemon juice · Food colouring (optional)

### FOR THE CARAMEL GLUE

200 g caster sugar · 150 ml water · Pastry brush

### TO DECORATE

Boiled sweets, for windows · Silver balls · Sweets, such as jelly beans or Smarties · Cinnamon sticks and/or chocolate fingers, for logs · Marshmallows, for snowmen, plus licorice 'laces' for their scarves · Lollies on sticks, and fruit pastilles on cocktail sticks, for trees or shrubs · Red and white candy canes, to dot around the garden · Icing sugar, for snow · Edible glitter and/or edible gold spray

1  Start by making your templates. Trace around the shapes on page 234, transfer them to card, then cut them out.

2  Preheat the oven to 200°C/Gas 6. Line two baking trays with parchment.

3  Put the butter, sugar and syrup into a large saucepan and melt over a medium heat.

4  Sift the flour, bicarbonate of soda and ginger into a large mixing bowl and pour in the butter mixture. Combine to form a firm dough. You can

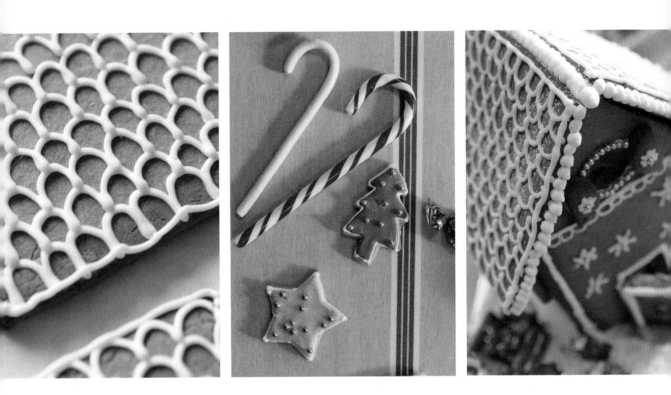

add a splash of water if necessary, but don't make it too wet. Form into a 20 cm circle, wrap in cling film and place in the fridge for 15 minutes.

5   Unwrap the chilled dough, place it between two large sheets of baking parchment and roll it out to a thickness of 1 cm. Remove the top sheet of parchment and discard it.

6   Place the roof template on the dough and cut around it with a small, sharp knife. Repeat with another roof panel, then transfer both to the baking trays, leaving a small gap between them.

7   Using the other templates, cut out a front wall, a back wall and two side walls. Cut out windows and a door as indicated, then transfer the walls and door to the baking sheets.

8   Place one or two boiled sweets in each window, depending on its size. They will melt during cooking and form the 'glass'.

9   Reroll the dough offcuts to make six rectangular shutters and four semicircular shutters by cutting around the appropriate templates. Any leftovers can be made into items

for the garden. We made biscuit stars, which we dotted around in the 'snow', and a four-sided tub that we filled with sweets, but you could make Christmas tree biscuits if you prefer. When all the shapes are on the baking trays, place in the oven for 10–12 minutes, or until just starting to turn darker at the edges and firm in the middle.

10   While the gingerbread is still on the trays, gently place the templates on the appropriate shapes and trim around the edges with a small, sharp knife to neaten them up as they will have expanded slightly during cooking. You need to work quite quickly before the gingerbread becomes too hard. Leave to cool completely before the next step.

### DECORATING THE HOUSE

11   The house is decorated with royal icing. To make this, lightly beat the egg white in a mixing bowl, then gradually add the icing sugar and lemon juice and beat until stiff and glossy. If the mixture is too stiff to mix, add a little more lemon juice (or even a little more egg white if it is *very* stiff). It should be thin enough to pipe

easily, but thick enough to hold its shape. It can also be coloured at this stage if you wish. If not using the icing straight away, cover with cling film to stop it drying out.

12 Place the roof panels with the narrow end nearest you. Spoon the icing into a piping bag fitted with a plain 3–4 mm nozzle and pipe a loop pattern that resembles roof tiles until both roof panels are covered. If you wish, you can put dots of icing along the edges of the roof.

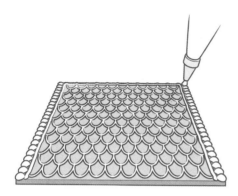

13 Decorate the front wall of the house with icing as you like. We outlined the edges of ours and piped stars, dotted with silver balls, but you could dot Smarties or jelly beans on it if you like, using a dab of icing to glue them in place. Don't forget the front door (although this will be separate from the house at the moment). Add a jelly bean or Smartie for the handle.

14 Pipe dots, squiggles or loops around the windows. On the back of the house (from which you haven't cut a door) pipe the outline of a window and decorate it in a similar way to the other windows.

15 Finally, pipe a star on each shutter and stick a silver ball in the middle. When all the decorating is done, let it dry thoroughly before the next step.

ASSEMBLING THE HOUSE

16 Prepare a cake board or something similar on which to assemble the house. A breadboard covered with foil would do.

17 The 'glue' that holds the house together is caramel, which is extremely hot, so handle it carefully. Pour the sugar and water into a heavy-based pan over a medium heat. Bring to the boil, swirling the pan gently to help dissolve the sugar, then boil for 5 minutes, or until the mixture has thickened and turned golden brown.

18 Place a jug in the middle of a silicone mat or plastic tray and prop three sides of the house against it: two tall sides opposite each other and the small side between them. Take a tall side, dip one edge into the hot caramel and stick to the short side next to it, making sure the edges are in contact all the way down. Repeat with the other tall side so you end up with the three sides attached to each other. You can now take the jug away and the structure should stand on its own.

19   Dip a pastry brush into the caramel and paint it along the unglued edges of the remaining short wall. Stick it to the tall walls. If more 'glue' is needed, apply it with a brush to the inside of the house so the exterior remains neat. Make sure the structure is sturdy before moving on to the roof.

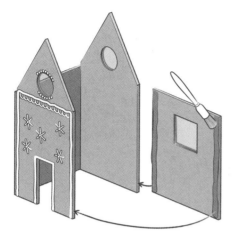

20   Lay one roof panel face down on the mat. Paint caramel along the top of the house's angled walls and along one short wall. Carefully place the glued edges on the roof panel and hold until firm. Repeat this process on the opposite side of the house to stick it to the remaining roof panel.

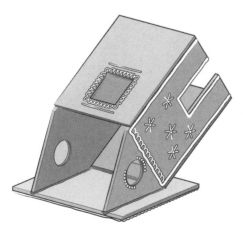

21   When the caramel has hardened, brush a little more caramel along the base of the walls, then very carefully stand the house up and position it on the cake board. Pipe some more icing along the visible joins of the house to hide the caramel bonding.

22   Brush caramel on the back of each shutter and stick in place on either side of each window.

23   Brush caramel along the 'hinge' edge of the front door and stick it to the house, opening outwards and slightly ajar, as if welcoming visitors in. Pipe some icing along the caramel to hide the join.

24   Decorate the garden with some of the sweet suggestions listed at the end of the ingredients. For example, use a mixture of chopped-up cinnamon sticks and/or chocolate fingers to make a pile of logs on either side of the front door; make marshmallow snowmen with licorice 'scarves', and dot them around; plant some lolly trees and fruit pastille shrubs in the garden. Just use your imagination.

25   Dust the roof and garden with icing sugar to look like freshly fallen snow, then sprinkle glitter where you wish. Oh, and edible gold spray also works brilliantly.

*To clean a pan that has hardened caramel stuck to it, add boiling water and simmer until the caramel has dissolved, then wash it straight away.*

*If you're pushed for time, you can buy gingerbread house kits where everything is pre-baked and cut for you and all you need to do is decorate.*

# PASSION FRUIT & COCONUT MARSHMALLOWS

I come from a marshmallow-obsessed household. Everybody in my life *loves* marshmallows because they combine three of their favourite things: skewers, fire and sweeties. These marshmallows make a brilliant edible gift that all ages can enjoy, and this wonderful recipe comes courtesy of Scott Paton, the head chef at the Horn of Plenty in Devon. I've cooked them up on several occasions and they always score me major Brownie points.

The great thing about this recipe is that you can flavour the marshmallows with practically anything. I've never tried alcohol, but it's on my list for when the kids aren't around to steal them. A final word of advice: make a couple of batches because I guarantee you'll eat most of what you planned to give away, so you'll need to start again the minute you finish.

## *YOU WILL NEED*

---

45 g leaf gelatine • 300 ml pure passion fruit juice (not concentrated), strained • 510 g honey • 675 g granulated sugar • 125 ml water • 500 g chocolate, broken into pieces • 500 g desiccated coconut, toasted

1  Soak the gelatine in a little cold water for about 10 minutes. Line a shallow 30 cm baking tray with foil.

2  Meanwhile, pour the fruit juice into a saucepan and simmer rapidly until reduced to 100 ml. This should take about 6 minutes on a high heat.

3  Put 210g of the honey in a saucepan with the sugar, water and reduced fruit juice. Boil until it reaches 110°C.

4  Squeeze out the gelatine, add it to the honey mixture and stir until dissolved. This is what gives marshmallow its unique texture.

5  Place the remaining honey in a bowl and pour the hot mixture over it and beat with an electric whisk until cool. As the mixture is boiling hot, start the beating slowly, then build up the speed and watch it change from orange to white. It should take around 8 minutes.

6  Pour the mixture into the prepared tray and leave to set in the fridge for 1 hour. After that, rest it at room temperature for 12 hours.

7  Cut the marshmallow into small squares with a hot, dry knife.

8  Melt the chocolate in a heatproof bowl set over a pan of simmering water (the boil must not actually touch it). Using a skewer, dip the marshmallows in the melted chocolate, then roll them in the desiccated coconut. Transfer to a plate and leave to set.

*Try using 100 ml of your favourite cordial instead of fresh fruit juice.*

*To make pretty gifts, pack the marshmallows in little boxes or cellophane bags and decorate the outside with string or ribbon and a gift tag.*

# THREE SPICE BLENDS

Yum, yum, yum in my tum, tum, tum. Or, if you're being the generous Christmas elf, add them to your hamper. These tasty spice blends by talented food writer Louisa Carter are heaven 'scent' in little jars.

---

## HOME-GROUND GARAM MASALA

Here's a tasty spice mixture that can be used in almost any Indian curry. Stir some into the onions at the beginning of cooking to add depth of flavour, and/or stir through at the end of cooking to add a more fragrant note. Garam masala can also be mixed with softened butter and rubbed onto a chicken before roasting. This recipe makes a 150 ml jar.

### YOU WILL NEED

- 2 tbsp black peppercorns
- 2 tbsp cumin seeds
- 4 tsp whole cloves
- 2 × 10 cm cinnamon sticks, broken into small pieces
- Seeds from 30 cardamom pods (bash the pods with a rolling pin to release the seeds)
- ½ a whole nutmeg (cover with a tea towel and bash with a rolling pin to break into pieces)

1  Place all the ingredients in a dry frying pan and over a low–medium heat for 3–4 minutes, stirring often, until lightly toasted and golden. Set aside to cool.

2  Transfer the toasted mixture to a spice grinder and grind to a powder. Store the mixture in a jar and seal tightly. It will keep for a month in a cool, dark place.

# WILD THYME ZAHTAR

Tangy and salty, this spice blend is fantastic sprinkled over grilled meats or chicken. It can also be mixed with extra virgin olive oil and drizzled over toasted flatbreads. The recipe makes a 150 ml jar.

YOU WILL NEED
- 5 tbsp white sesame seeds
- 3 tbsp dried thyme, oregano or marjoram (preferably wild)
- 2 tbsp ground sumac (a lemony spice available from Middle Eastern shops)
- 1 tsp flaked sea salt

1  Place the sesame seeds in a frying pan over a low–medium heat for 3–4 minutes, stirring often, until lightly toasted and golden. Set aside to cool completely.

2  Using a spice grinder or mortar and pestle, coarsely grind the sesame seeds and thyme (or the oregano of marjoram, if you prefer), leaving plenty of texture and a few whole seeds. Stir in the sumac and salt. Store the mixture in a jar and seal tightly. It will keep for a month in a cool, dark place.

# RAS EL HANOUT
## WITH ROSE PETALS

This is a heady Moroccan spice blend that can be stirred through any tagine or stew, and is particularly good with lamb, quail or fish. You can also add it to couscous, stir it through grilled or roasted vegetables, or rub it into lamb or fish before grilling. The recipe makes a 150 ml jar.

YOU WILL NEED
- 4 tbsp dried edible rose petals (available at Middle Eastern food stores and online)
- 1 tsp dried lavender (optional)
- 2 tsp turmeric powder
- 1 tsp ground ginger

FOR THE TOASTED MIXTURE
- 6 dried red chillies (Kashmiri are good), stalks snipped off
- 15 cm cinnamon stick, broken into small pieces
- 1 tbsp whole cloves
- 1 tbsp coriander seeds
- 1 tbsp cumin seeds
- 1 tbsp fennel seeds
- ¼ nutmeg (cover with a tea towel and bash with a rolling pin to break a whole nutmeg into pieces)

1  Place all the ingredients for toasting in a frying pan over a low–medium heat for 3–4 minutes, stirring often, until lightly toasted and fragrant. Set aside to cool.

2  Transfer the toasted mixture to a spice grinder, add 3 tablespoons of the rose petals and all the lavender (if using), then grind to a powder. Stir in the turmeric, ginger and remaining rose petals. Store the mixture in a jar and seal tightly. It will keep for a month in a cool, dark place.

# CHRISTMAS MENDIANTS

*Mendiants* are a traditional French confectionery made as part of the thirteen Christmas desserts of the Provence region. Personally, I can't think of anything better than thirteen Christmas desserts. In the past the custom was to top them with raisins, hazelnuts, dried figs and almonds to represent the four main monastic orders of the Dominicans, Augustinians, Franciscans and Carmelites. Nowadays, they're topped with all manner of fruit and nut delights. Artisan chocolatier Suzie Read of Big Ridge Chocolates, based in the glorious Highlands of Scotland, has made *mendiants* one of her Christmas specialities. Her most popular topping combo is toasted cashews, dried cranberries and a piece of crystallised ginger on a plain chocolate base. Yum!

*Mendiants* are a perfect last-minute gift or a delicious after-dinner sweet. Using plain, milk or white chocolate, and adding the toppings of your choice, allows you to tailor them for a particular person. Thank you, Suzie!

## YOU WILL NEED

About 60 g whole cashew nuts · 400 g good-quality plain chocolate, finely chopped · About 30 g dried cranberries · About 40 g crystallised ginger

1 Preheat the oven to 180°C/Gas 4. Line two baking trays with greaseproof paper or silicone baking mats.

2 Scatter your cashews in a single layer on a baking tray and roast in the oven for 5–8 minutes, stirring them halfway through. Set aside to cool.

3 Melt 320 g of the chocolate in a heatproof bowl set over a pan of simmering water (the bowl must not touch the water). Stir occasionally until just melted, then take the pan off the heat and add the remaining 80 g of 'seed' chocolate

(see box opposite). Allow it to melt in the residual heat, stirring with a spatula or spoon.

4 When the chocolate is fully melted, remove the bowl from the pan and wipe the bottom dry to avoid any drips mixing with the chocolate. Keep your pan of water warm in case you need it for reheating the chocolate a little later.

5 Using a teaspoon, pour little discs of melted chocolate onto the prepared trays and use the back of the spoon to spread them to the size of a 50p coin. Do about four at a time because the toppings must be added while the chocolate is

still soft. Gently press one cashew nut, two or three pieces of dried cranberry and one piece of ginger onto the top of each chocolate circle.

6  Continue making *mendiants* in the same way until your trays are full. If the chocolate in your bowl begins to thicken a little before you have finished, just pop it back on top of the pan of warm water and stir until liquid again. Allow the *mendiants* to set in a cool, dry place for 2–3 hours. Pop the chocolates into gift boxes or bags, tie with a ribbon and share them – although it's tempting to keep them all to yourself.

Mendiants *can be made up to two weeks in advance if stored in an airtight container in a cool, dry place.*

### TEMPERING CHOCOLATE

I've had a go at chocolatiering before, and quickly learnt that it requires some patience because the chocolate doesn't like to be rushed or get too hot. There are lots of different ways to temper chocolate, which basically means letting it melt at the correct temperature so that it sets with a lovely gloss, a good snap and no streaks, also known as 'bloom', but not a good bloom.

One of the simplest ways for a beginner to temper chocolate is to add 'seed' chocolate to just melted chocolate (as we did in step 3). This is not the exact science of tempering (which requires chocolate thermometers), but if done slowly, it should give great results.

# LIMONCELLO

You can't go wrong with this classic recipe for homemade Limoncello. It should keep around six months, although it doesn't last six days in my house! It makes a fantastic gift, but it's definitely worth making some for your own Christmas drinks cabinet too.

## YOU WILL NEED

———————

Zest and juice of 8 unwaxed lemons  ·  800 g granulated sugar  ·
650 ml water  ·  1 litre vodka

1  Place the lemon zest in a large pan with the sugar and water. Heat gently until the sugar dissolves, then increase the heat slightly and simmer for 15 minutes.

2  Take the pan off the heat, add the lemon juice and vodka, then cover and leave the liquid to infuse for a week.

3  Using a sieve lined with muslin or kitchen paper, strain the liquid into a large jug. Decant into sterilised bottles (see page 138), seal tightly and add a pretty label.

# FOOD & DRINK

---

## TRADITIONAL AND MODERN
## CHRISTMAS FARE

For me, Christmas is as much about feasting as it is about gifts and decorations and if there is one meal I look forward to above all others it's Christmas dinner.

At the risk of sounding like a broken record, a successful (stress-free) Christmas lunch does boil down to preparation. My advice for anyone in charge of the day's proceedings is to sit down well in advance with a large piece of paper, write down the names of everyone coming, plan your menu (think homemade and hearty – fancy food at Christmas is more hassle than it's worth), work out who should do what, who should bring what and what you need to order in advance, such as the meat or fish. These basic rules don't just apply to Christmas Day; they work for all parties and gatherings. Sharing the workload and the costs of Christmas lunch with everyone coming is definitely a good plan.

In my family, we all have different jobs depending on whose house we're going to. On one occasion I was put in charge of the main meat dish, so I made James Mackenzie's rib of beef on page 167. I was terrified it would be a disaster, but I needn't have feared – James's recipe didn't fail me, and the rib of beef was a massive hit with everyone.

Phil Spencer always gives me a ham from Farmer Guy in Kent, which usually arrives around 22 December. A couple of years ago there was a huge snowfall just before Christmas and I feared the ham wouldn't make it through, but I'm very pleased to say it has never let me down. The recipe for the ham can be found on page 164. In my opinion, you can't beat ham and eggs on Boxing Day morning.

Many dishes can be prepared a day or two in advance and kept in the fridge. These include the bread sauce and the cranberry sauce. Most of the meat work can usually be done the day before as well. The Christmas pudding and cake on pages 174 and 177 can be made several weeks in advance, of course, and the mincemeat on page 170 can be kept for a month in the fridge, or twice that in a sealed jar. If you don't have enough fridge space to squeeze in all the stuff you make in advance, put it in well-sealed containers in a cold garage or shed. Don't do this with your meat, though; you must make space for that in the fridge.

Roast potatoes can be par-boiled, drained and bashed around in the pan (important for roasting), then left to cool and kept chilled overnight before you roast them the following day. Now, 'roast potato-gate' is an annual occurrence in my family, so I'll leave it up to you to decide how you want to do yours. My brother Henry and my sister Sofie have very different approaches. Henry favours goose fat, whereas Sofie is adamant that olive oil is the way forward. Natasha reckons they're both hot and crunchy and is equally pleased with either version. Whether using oil or fat simply, heat it in a heavy-based roasting tin that will fit all your potatoes in a single layer. When smoking hot, add the potatoes, turning them to coat evenly, and roast for 40–60 minutes, turning once, until they're really crispy and golden and perfectly fluffy in the middle.

We always have Stilton cheese at Christmas, and the job of getting it belongs to my other half. He takes great pride in presenting it beautifully, using his collection of old butter and cheese dishes, and a pair of Stilton ceramic towers he bought at auction, so the cheese always looks splendid.

While wine and bubbly play an important part in the celebrations, I've become a dab hand at making cocktails because they're such fun and help things to go with a swing. You'll need a few key tools, including a shaker, a strainer and a lemon press. Try the delicious tipples on page 189 – they're perfect for a party. If you've got a big crowd coming, I recommend the mulled cider (see page 186).

Please remember, there is nothing wrong with buying a few ready-made goodies that you spruce up with, say, extra herbs or icing sugar, and present in nice serving dishes. My family believes that the only bread sauce worth having is from a packet. There are also some delicious stuffings available in the shops.

Whatever you're planning, I hope your Christmas Day will be spent eating, drinking and making very, very merry with the people you love most.

# GLAZED HAM

I love the ham Phil gives me: it's absolutely delicious and big enough to feed a small army, so it lasts way beyond Christmas Day. A few years ago, when we were making *Kirstie and Phil's Perfect Christmas*, we asked Farmer Guy if he'd let us in on the secrets of making one of his glorious hams and he kindly agreed.

The ham we cooked weighed 7 kg and required a giant pot. If that's too big for your needs, buy something smaller and reduce the other ingredients proportionately. The key is to poach it in enough liquid to cover the ham. For years since we made it on the show, I've had messages from people all over who have made it too and it's been an utter success. It serves at least 12, and there are generous leftovers.

## YOU WILL NEED

---

7 kg unsmoked ham joint · 1 part cider · 1 part apple juice · 1 part water · 1 tbsp cloves · 2 cinnamon sticks · 6 apples, halved

### FOR THE GLAZE
225 g dark brown sugar · 225 g honey · 1 tsp English mustard powder · 1 tbsp wholegrain mustard · Sprinkling of cloves · 1 cinnamon stick · Spiced cider (enough to wet the other ingredients) · Splash of cider vinegar

### TO GARNISH
Glacé cherries, halved · Cloves

---

1  Place the ham in a large saucepan. Combine equal parts of the cider, apple juice and water until you have enough liquid to cover the ham. Add the cloves, cinnamon and apples, then bring to the boil. Cover and simmer for about 1 hour per kilogram.

2  Once cooked, drain the ham and set aside until cool enough to handle. At that point, remove the skin, leaving just a thin layer of fat on the joint.

3  Preheat the oven to 180°C/Gas 4. Score the fat into a diamond pattern (this will release the ham's flavour and help it absorb the glaze), then place the joint in the oven for just 10 minutes to let it crisp up.

4  Meanwhile, put all the glaze ingredients, except the vinegar, into a saucepan. Bring to the boil, then add the vinegar and stir well.

5  Spoon the hot glaze over the ham, then return it to the oven for 10 minutes. Repeat the glazing and roasting process two or three times, until the ham looks well coated and is done to your taste.

6  To garnish the ham, place the glacé cherries on alternate diamonds, securing them in place with cloves.

*Ham is divine with my niece Nancy's parsley sauce. Simply make a roux with 20 g butter and 20 g flour in a pan. Add about 200 ml milk, lots of chopped parsley and a squeeze of lemon juice. The sauce should be quite runny. Season well with salt and pepper.*

# MUSTARD-CRUSTED RIB OF BEEF
## WITH BUBBLE & SQUEAK CAKES

I first met Michelin-starred chef James Mackenzie of the Pipe & Glass Inn in East Yorkshire when I was competing in the needlecraft competition at the Great Yorkshire Show. The highlight of that day wasn't winning first prize for my appliquéd cushion (although that was pretty cool); it was taking part in a cookery demonstration, where James taught me the best, most simple and delicious way of making Yorkshire puddings I've ever encountered. He then agreed to come to Meadowgate and helped me make this amazing rib of beef (a great alternative to turkey) as my contribution to a local Christmas fair. It has since become a family favourite because of its simplicity and incredible taste. It's no wonder that beef was the Christmas joint of choice in Britain until the 17th century, when King James I thought turkey would be better for his digestion.

The bubble and squeak cakes and mulled wine gravy are perfect accompaniments. The quantities below serve 8–10. Enjoy!

## *YOU WILL NEED*

---

5 kg rib of beef · Rapeseed oil · 4 carrots, washed and roughly chopped · 2 onions, peeled and roughly chopped · 2 leeks, washed and roughly chopped · 2 celery sticks, washed and roughly chopped · 4 tbsp English mustard · 4 tbsp Dijon mustard · 4 tbsp wholegrain mustard

### FOR THE BUBBLE AND SQUEAK CAKES
Rapeseed oil · 1 large onion, peeled and sliced · 300 g cooked Brussels sprouts, sliced · Handful of curly kale, shredded · 200 g cooked chestnuts · 100 g bacon lardons, fried until crisp · 6 fresh sage leaves · 1 kg dry mashed potato · Plain flour, for shaping the cakes · 100 g butter

### FOR THE MULLED WINE GRAVY
2 large onions, peeled and sliced · 4 glasses mulled wine · 2 tbsp plain flour · 1 litre beef stock · 2 tbsp redcurrant jelly · Salt and pepper

---

1 Preheat the oven to 160°C/Gas 3. Clean the bones on the rib of beef, then sear the joint in a hot roasting tray with a little rapeseed oil until golden brown all over.

2 Transfer the rib of beef to a plate, then place the carrots, onions, leeks and celery in the roasting tray.

3 Mix all three mustards in a bowl and rub the mixture all over the meat. Cover the exposed bones with foil.

4 Place the beef on the vegetables, cover the whole tray with foil and roast in the oven for 1 hour. Remove the foil and continue roasting for a further 1½ hours.

5 To make the bubble and squeak cakes, heat a little rapeseed oil in a frying pan and cook the onion for about 10 minutes, until translucent. Add the sprouts, kale, chestnuts and bacon and cook for a further 2 minutes. Set aside to cool.

6 Add the cooled veg mixture and the sage leaves to the mashed potato. Dust your hands with flour and shape the mixture into little cakes. Transfer to a plate and place in the fridge to set for at least 30 minutes.

7 Meanwhile, place the onions and half the mulled wine for the gravy in a large saucepan over a high heat and bring to the boil. Lower the heat and simmer for 30 minutes.

8 When the beef is cooked, transfer it to a warmed serving plate, cover loosely with foil and a tea towel and leave to rest for 30 minutes. Pour the excess oil out of the roasting tray, then set it aside with the roasted veg still inside it.

9 To cook the bubble and squeak cakes, heat the butter and a little rapeseed oil in a large frying pan and fry the cakes until brown on both sides.

10 Place the tray of roasted veg over the heat, add the flour and cook, stirring, for 2 minutes. Pour in the remaining mulled wine and beef stock, scraping up any bits stuck to the bottom of the tray, then bring to the boil and simmer for 3–4 minutes. Strain the gravy through a sieve into the pan of cooked onion and mulled wine, using the back of a spoon to push all the flavour out of the vegetables. Stir in the redcurrant jelly, check the seasoning and serve with the beef and bubble and squeak cakes.

# MINCEMEAT & MINCE PIES

Christmas just wouldn't be Christmas without a mince pie or three. With homemade mincemeat and light-as-air filo pastry, you might want even more than three!

---

## HOMEMADE MINCEMEAT

Here's an easy, delicious recipe from Victoria Cranfield that doesn't take at all long to prepare. The mincemeat can be made just the day before, or up to two months in advance if stored in a sealed jar in the fridge. It also makes a lovely addition to a gift hamper.

Victoria's tip is to always use the best ingredients you can afford as the difference in taste really is noticeable. The recipe makes about 1 kg.

**YOU WILL NEED**

- 227 g sultanas, chopped
- 227 g raisins, chopped
- 1½ packets (about 227 g) ready-to-eat dates, pitted and chopped
- 120 g glacé cherries, chopped
- 60 g walnuts, chopped
- 25 g piece of fresh root ginger, peeled
- 2 tbsp honey
- 1 tbsp cider vinegar
- About 130 g good Seville marmalade
- 1 tsp powdered allspice
- 120 ml brandy
- Zest and juice of 2 oranges
- 120 g shredded suet (vegetarian if you wish)

1  Chop the dried fruit and walnuts to the size that suits you and place in a bowl. If you'd like a smoother texture, simply mince the fruit in a food processor instead.

2  Chop the ginger into tiny little cubes (this gives a better result than grating it) and add to the fruit mixture.

3  Put the honey and vinegar in a measuring jug, add 300 ml boiling water and stir until the honey melts. Pour it into the fruit mixture, stir well, then set aside to cool.

4  Add the marmalade to the fruit (the peel can be finely chopped first if you wish), then mix in all the remaining ingredients. Cover and leave over night.

5  Sterilise all your jars and lids as described on page 138.

6  Stir the fruit mixture, adding a little more brandy if it seems too dry. Pack it tightly into the prepared jars – you don't want any air bubbles – and seal tightly. If reusing lids, place a brandy-dipped wax paper circle on the surface of the mincemeat. If not using the mincemeat straight away, label and date the jars.

# FILO MINCE PIES

Although shortcrust pastry is traditionally used for mince pies, filo makes a lovely lighter alternative. Top the pies off with a sprinkle of edible glitter for some extra sparkle. This recipes makes 24.

## YOU WILL NEED

- 100 g melted butter
- 1 × 270 g packet filo pastry
- 1 quantity homemade mincemeat (see above)
- Icing sugar, for dusting
- Ground cinnamon, for dusting
- Edible glitter, to decorate

1  Preheat the oven to 200°C/Gas 6. Brush two 12-hole mince pie tins with a little of the melted butter.

2  Lay a sheet of filo on a board (cover the remaining pastry with a damp tea towel while you work to stop it drying out). Brush the sheet all over with melted butter, then cut into 12 squares slightly larger than the holes in the tin. Repeat as necessary until you have 72 squares.

3  Place a square in each hole. Then insert a second square at an angle so that the corners do not align. The arrangement should look like a star shape from above.

4  Spoon a teaspoonful of mincemeat into each pastry case (don't be too generous or the pies will be soggy and oversweet). Cover each with a scrunched-up square of filo.

5  Bake in the oven for 10–12 minutes, until golden. Cool in the tin for a minute or two, then transfer to a wire rack. Dust the pies with icing sugar and cinnamon and sprinkle with edible glitter. Serve warm or cold.

———————

*If you want a lighter mincemeat, add a little stewed apple to it just before use.*

*Omit the suet if making the mincemeat for people who are gluten-intolerant, and instead mix in a little grated butter before use.*

———————

# CHRISTMAS PUDDING

Dense, dark, and heavy with booze, Christmas pudding is the crowning glory of the festive season. I'm a massive fan. It was traditionally made on 'Stir-up Sunday', around five weeks before Christmas, so it had enough time to mature and develop its full, rich flavour. Each family member would give it a stir and make a wish, and various items were added: silver coins (for wealth), wishbones (for good luck), a silver thimble (for thrift), and a ring (for marriage). If you're a traditionalist, you can buy sterling silver Christmas pudding charms online.

Food writer Louisa Carter's recipe makes a 1.2 litre pudding, which serves 6–8. It can be made and served straight away, or left to mature for a couple of months.

## YOU WILL NEED

150 g dried sour cherries and/or dried cranberries  ·  300 g mixed dried fruit (raisins, sultanas, finely chopped dates)  ·  75 ml brandy  ·  Juice and grated zest of 1 orange  ·  100 g softened butter, plus extra for greasing  ·  115 g dark muscovado sugar  ·  2 large eggs, lightly beaten  ·  75 g self-raising flour  · 55 g fresh white breadcrumbs  ·  50 g chopped pecan nuts  ·  1 tsp mixed spice

1  Place the dried fruit in a saucepan with the brandy, orange zest and juice. Bring to a simmer, then turn the heat off, cover the pan with a lid and leave to steep for 30 minutes.

2  Lightly grease a 1.2–1.4 litre pudding basin with melted butter and place a circle of greaseproof paper in the bottom. Cut 2 sheets of greaseproof paper and 2 sheets of foil each measuring roughly 35 × 35cm. Set aside.

3  Put the butter and sugar into a large mixing bowl and beat together until pale and fluffy.

4  Whisk in the eggs one at a time, adding a spoonful of flour between each one if the mixture starts to curdle.

5  Add the soaked fruit and all the juices and stir well to combine. Gently fold in the flour, breadcrumbs, nuts and mixed spice.

6  Spoon the mixture into the prepared basin and smooth the top with a spatula.

7  Place the two sheets of greaseproof on top of the two sheets of foil and make a pleat about 4 cm wide down the middle – this is to allow for expansion during cooking. Place it over the pudding basin and tie securely with string, making a loop over the top to act as a handle. Trim off any excess paper and foil, or roll it up tightly – it's very important that the greaseproof doesn't come into contact with the water during cooking as it could make the pudding soggy.

8 Put a trivet, upturned cake tin or dariole mould in a large saucepan and sit the basin on it. Carefully pour in 5–7 cm boiling water so it comes just below the basin but doesn't actually touch it. Cover the pan with a lid and steam the pudding for 4 hours, topping up the water now and again, as necessary.

9 If not serving the pudding straight away, set it aside to cool completely, then rewrap it in fresh greaseproof paper and foil and store in a cool dark place for up to 2 months. To serve, reheat by steaming for 2 hours.

# CHRISTMAS CAKE

I love this recipe by the amazing Rosie Davies. She's not only a brilliant cook, but also an inspiring teacher full of tricks and ideas. For example, she taught me that when adding treacle to something, first grease the spoon with vegetable oil and it will slide off without leaving any sticky trail. Genius!

This is very much a 'chuck it in' type of recipe. I like to use tons and tons of stem ginger, so I add more than listed, but you might prefer extra cherries or apricots: the choice is yours. One of the best things about this cake is that you don't have to make it months in advance of Christmas. You can knock it together the day before you're having guests and decorate it with almonds and a dusting of sugar. If you do want to go the whole hog with marzipan and icing, allow a couple of days extra.

One final thing: don't limit yourself to making this cake just at Christmas; it's also lovely during the summer with iced tea and coffee.

## *YOU WILL NEED*

---

900 g of your favourite mixed dried fruit (dates, prunes, apricots, sultanas, currants, stem ginger), or you can use a packet of mixed dried fruit, all washed and dried on a clean cloth • 300 ml dry cider • 225 g butter • 225 g soft brown sugar • Juice and finely grated rind of 1 lemon and 1 orange • 1 tbsp black treacle (optional) • 4 large eggs, beaten • 225 g plain flour • 1 tsp ground mixed spice • ½ tsp ground nutmeg • 170 g chopped mixed nuts (almonds, hazelnuts, pecans) • Whole almonds and demerara sugar, for decoration (if not icing the cake) • About 6 tbsp apple brandy (ordinary brandy or whisky could be used instead)

### FOR THE MARZIPAN (OPTIONAL)
225 g ground almonds • 180 g caster sugar • 110 g icing sugar, plus extra for dusting • 1 large egg, beaten • 1 tbsp alcohol (could be more apple brandy) • A few drops of whatever flavouring you fancy, e.g. vanilla extract, rose water or orange flower water

### FOR THE APRICOT GLAZE (OPTIONAL)
½ jar cheap apricot jam • Juice of 1 lemon

1 kg icing sugar · 3–4 egg whites · 1–2 tbsp glycerine (available from chemists and supermarkets; stops the icing drying rock hard, and the amount added depends on how hard or soft you want it to be) · Juice of ½ lemon · Cake-top decorations, such as holly

---

1  Preheat the oven to 150°C/Gas 2. Line a 20 cm cake tin with two layers of greaseproof paper. Make sure the paper around the sides goes about 5 cm above the rim of the tin so that none of the mixture escapes as it rises.

2  Chop up the larger pieces of dried fruit so that they're about the same size as the sultanas and currants.

3  Put all the fruit in a pan with the cider, bring to the boil and simmer for 2–3 minutes. Set aside and allow to get cold. The fruit should absorb all the liquid, but drain off any that's left.

4  Cream the butter and sugar in a large mixing bowl. Add the orange and lemon zest, then the treacle, if using (it's great for flavour and colour, but if it's not to your taste, it can be left out). Pour in the beaten eggs and mix well.

5  Sift in the flour, mixed spice and nutmeg and fold them into the egg mixture.

6  Now stir in the soaked fruit mixture, the chopped nuts and some of the citrus juices to produce a mixture that has a soft dropping consistency.

7  Spoon the mixture into the prepared tin, smooth the top, then make a shallow hollow in the middle so that the cake will rise evenly as it cooks. If you are *not* going to ice the cake, arrange the whole almonds over the surface and add a sprinkling of demerara sugar to give a lovely crunchy topping.

8  Wrap a thick layer of brown paper or newspaper around the outside of the tin – as high as the lining paper – and secure with string. (The paper will prevent the cake edges from burning.) Place the tin on a baking tray lined with more brown paper and bake for 3–4 hours. Check the cake halfway through the baking time – if the top is getting too brown, cover it with a piece of brown paper.

9  Check that the cake is cooked by inserting a skewer in the middle – it should come out clean. Remove the cake from the oven, prick it all over with a fine skewer and carefully pour the apple brandy into the holes. Allow the cake to cool completely before removing it from the tin (usually around 2 hours).

10  To make the marzipan, sift the dry ingredients together. Add the egg, alcohol and flavouring and mix until you have a pastry-like consistency. Knead until smooth (not too long or it will go oily), then wrap tightly in cling film. Set aside to rest in a cool place for at least 1 hour.

11  Place a large piece of cling film on a clean work surface and sift a generous amount of icing sugar over it. Put the chilled marzipan in the middle of the cling film and roll into a circle that is big enough to cover the top and sides of the cake. Use a pastry brush to remove all excess icing sugar.

12  To make the glaze, put the jam and lemon juice in a saucepan, heat until combined, then sieve to remove the bits. Return the glaze to the pan and continue to simmer until thick.

13  Turn the cake upside down and brush the bottom of it with the glaze. Place it glaze side down on the marzipan. Press down lightly to make sure it sticks, then carefully brush the sides of the cake with more glaze, being careful not to slop it over the marzipan.

14  Take a deep breath and lift both the cling film and marzipan up all around the cake and smooth it onto the sides of the cake through the film. Make sure it sticks properly.

15  With the cling film still in place, turn the cake over and press it firmly all over with your hands. Peel off the film, then trim off any excess marzipan and, if necessary, glue any loose areas with more glaze.

16  Place the cake on a board and roll a straight-sided jam jar around the sides to get a really flat vertical surface. If necessary, dust with a little more icing sugar. Allow to dry out overnight, or even longer if possible.

17  To make the icing, sift the icing sugar into a large bowl. Put the egg whites into a separate bowl and whisk until foamy. Gradually add the sifted icing sugar to the eggs, whisking slowly at first as the sugar will go everywhere like a cloud of talcum powder if you mix too fast. Add the glycerine and lemon juice, then beat hard until the mixture is smooth and shiny. It should be the consistency of plaster of Paris.

18  Press cling film directly onto the surface of the icing and set aside for several hours to allow the air bubbles to come out.

19  When you're ready to apply the icing, place the cake on a turntable, or centre the board on a large saucepan that you can turn to get good coverage. Using a palette knife, spread the icing on the sides of the cake, occasionally dipping the blade in a jug of hot water to make the spreading easier. Ideally, allow the sides to dry overnight before icing the top.

20  Add any cake-top decorations, such as a sprig of holly, an hour or so after icing, before the surface sets hard. For the perfect finish, tie one of Jane Means' flat bows around your cake (see page 73).

*The hollow created in the raw cake can be made with the back of a wooden spoon or a damp hand.*

*Make the icing and the marzipan as soon as the cake is in the oven so that they can rest as long as possible before you need to use them.*

*If you want to use ready-made marzipan, Rosie recommends the white kind, but it doesn't taste nearly as good as homemade.*

*It's possible to buy ready-made sheets of royal icing for the cake, but this cake is so good that I'd recommend making your own.*

*Make sure the cake is completely cold before applying the marzipan and icing. If done when still warm, the cake might crumble and the marzipan could melt into a sticky mess.*

*The best way to store fruit cakes is wrapped in greaseproof paper in an airtight tin.*

# YULE LOG

Traditionally, the Yule log was exactly that – a wooden log set in the fireplace on Christmas Eve and that was large enough to burn throughout the twelve days of Christmas. It was thought to bring prosperity and ward off evil for the coming year. A few Christmases ago my good luck arrived in the form of chef Richard Hunt, who taught me how to make a delicious edible version of the yule log. I had never made one before and, to be honest, I don't think I'd ever actually eaten one. I remember them being everywhere in the 1970s, but then they fell out of favour until quite recently, when they became chic again.

I made mine to enter the yule log competition at Jo Colwill's Cowslip Workshops Christmas Fair and it won first prize. Yes, remember that time I did that crazy, crazy summer of country show competitions? Well, it carried into the winter, and I went up against all my fellow competitors in this grand finale. I'm still recovering. In fact, someone asked me just the other day how to make a yule log that didn't crack, and I said I didn't know because *I* almost cracked making it. Then I remembered the secret weapon was ganache – the thick chocolate covering that heals and hides all manner of broken sponge bits – and I recalled that really it's supposed to look like an old wooden log, rather than a perfect Swiss roll.

Richard was my walking, talking recipe book, but when it came to decorating the log, I was on my own, and I went way overboard with my icing sugar snow. There was a point where it looked like an avalanche had hit, so I had to take it outside and wait for a strong gust of wind to blow some away. Not good, because the winter wind was strong and my log came close to hitting the ground, which would have been a disaster. It did come together in the end, though, and it was great fun to make. I'm sure it will get your creative juices flowing.

## YOU WILL NEED

---

45 g hot melted butter, plus extra for greasing  •  45 g plain flour  •
35 g good-quality cocoa powder  •  4 eggs  •  100 g caster sugar

### FOR THE FILLING
200 ml double cream  •  20 g caster sugar  •  1 vanilla pod  •  75 g cherries in
Kirsch, chopped

340 ml double cream  •  250 g dark chocolate (at least 70% cocoa solids),
broken into pieces  •  50 g chestnut purée

Chocolate leaves  •  Marzipan, to make holly and berries  •  Red and green
food colouring (optional)  •  Icing sugar

---

1 Preheat the oven to 190°C/Gas 5. Grease a 23 × 38 cm Swiss roll tin and line the bottom and the sides with baking parchment.

2 Sift the flour and cocoa powder together three times, then set aside.

3 Place the eggs in a saucepan and whisk in the sugar. Place over a gentle heat and whisk constantly until the mixture is warm and foamy. Pour into a bowl and whisk at a high speed until the mixture is no longer foaming and the bubbles have disappeared. When it is thick, rich and has tripled in volume, whisk at the lowest speed for 1 minute, until the mixture leaves a trail for a short while after the beaters are lifted.

4 Sift the flour mixture over the egg mixture and gently fold together until thoroughly combined. Do not overmix.

5 Pour 2 tablespoonfuls of the egg and flour mixture into the melted butter and fold together. Add to the remaining cake mix and gently fold together again.

6 Pour the cake batter into the prepared tin, tilting it to spread evenly, then tap it sharply against the work surface several times to burst any air bubbles.

7 Bake in the middle of the oven for 10–15 minutes, until the cake springs back when touched gently, and a skewer inserted into the centre comes out dry. Set aside to cool slightly, then carefully invert it onto fresh parchment sprinkled with icing sugar. (Don't do what I did and throw it out.) Peel off the paper, then roll up the cake and fresh paper together. Don't worry if the sponge cracks as you do this; that's what happens. Leave it to cool.

8 To make the filling, whip the cream until stiff, then gently fold in the sugar, vanilla and cherries. Don't do this in a machine.

9 Unroll your sponge and spread the filling evenly over it, leaving a 2 cm clear border at one short end. Starting with that border, roll the cake up again, this time without the paper.

10 Cut a wedge off one end of the log and flatten it slightly into a thick, more rectangular shape. Place it beside the log at a 45-degree angle so it looks like a branch sticking out of the trunk. Chill for 30 minutes.

11 Meanwhile, make the ganache. Whip 200 ml of the cream until thick. Place the chocolate in a separate heatproof bowl. Bring the rest of the cream to the boil, then pour it over the chocolate. Mix until smooth, then gently fold in the whipped cream and chestnut purée.

12 Spread the ganache all over the chilled cake and make ridges with a fork to give it a bark-like appearance. Don't forget to swirl the ends to create the illusion of tree rings.

13 Decorate with the chocolate leaves (see Tips) and marzipan holly, then dust with icing sugar. Serve at room temperature.

If you want to create an even more bark-like texture, paint a thin layer of melted chocolate onto a sheet of baking parchment and place in the fridge until set. Break it into shards and stick them to your log.

The same melted chocolate technique can be used to make leaves; just cut them out of the chocolate sheet with a sharp knife.

# MULLED CIDER

Andy Thompstone of Thompstone's Devonshire Cider showed me how to make this mulled cider at Jo Colwill's Christmas Craft Fair and it went down a treat. This recipe makes 8-litres, but you can reduce the ingredients proportionately. It's a great opening tipple for a pre-Christmas drinks party – it will certainly warm everyone's cockles.

## YOU WILL NEED

8 litres good-quality dry cider · 56 g ground cassia or 3 crushed cinnamon sticks · 2 tbsp allspice berries, crushed · 2 tsp ground star anise · 2 tsp ground cloves · 2 tbsp peeled and grated fresh root ginger · 2 pinches ground nutmeg · 286 g dark muscovado sugar (less if using sweet cider) · Rum, to taste (around ¼ bottle)

1 Pour the cider into a large, heavy-based pan and warm over a medium heat.

2 Add all the spices and sugar, then carefully bring the mixture up to 60°C. If you go over that, you run the risk of boiling off the alcohol.

3 Take the pan off the heat, cover with a lid and allow to steep for at least a few hours. The longer you leave it, the spicier the drink.

4 Add as much rum as you dare, then sieve the liquid to get rid of the spices. Your cider is now ready to drink. Simply reheat and enjoy.

# COCKTAILS

Someone once asked me what, out of all the things I've learnt to make on the craft shows, do I use most in my day-to-day life. The truth is cocktails. At the risk of sounding like a total lush, I'm now the proud owner of a decent kit that includes a shaker, a strainer and the cocktail's trusty friend, a lemon press, which would make a great Christmas present for any friends who, like me, are rather partial to a cocktail. You can shop around online and read up on all the different equipment essentials to get started.

If you come to my house for a party these days, you'll be given more than a G&T. If all else fails, I'm thinking a career at Raffles hotel in Singapore could be my next stop. I like creating my own concoctions, but I've also got recipe books and I enjoy looking for ideas online. I recently read that a great way to learn how to make a good cocktail is to make your own lemonade because the basis of the craft is about understanding the relationship between strong (the big alcohol component, such as vodka) and weak (the minor alcohol, such as a liqueur), and sour (mainly citrus fruits) and sweet (such as sugar and syrups). When making homemade lemonade, you can experiment with the base layer of sour and sweet in just the same way to suit your taste.

The history of the cocktail is a long-disputed one. Americans will swear blind that it was their invention. However, there is mounting evidence in favour of far more British roots. The *Daily Telegraph* found the word 'cocktail' used in a March 1798 edition of the *Morning Post and Gazeteer*, a long-obsolete London newspaper, when it ran a satirical article listing who in British politics owed what at the Axe & Gate tavern. Apparently, William Pitt the Younger's bar tab included a 'cock-tail, vulgarly called ginger'. Search online to see the article – it's brilliant reading.

The number one tip Phil and I were given by Joe McCanta, who made cocktails with us on *Kirstie & Phil's Perfect Christmas*, was ice, baby. It's what makes the difference between a great cocktail and a bad one.

Starting a cocktail cabinet is pretty cool, and adding to the collection can become quite addictive. But the best thing of all is experimenting and having fun.

———

# ORANGE CHRISTMAS CREAM

This is the perfect cocktail for all that cream liqueur you've had hanging around the cupboard.

YOU WILL NEED
- Cream liqueur
- Orange peel
- Fresh nutmeg (*so* Christmassy)

1  Pour a good lug of cream liqueur into your cocktail shaker – it should be about a third full.

2  Using a potato peeler, cut a thick strip of orange peel and squeeze the oil from it into the shaker. Add the peel itself and fill the rest of the shaker with ice.

3  Put the lid on and shake like a cocktail-maker should. The shaking cools and slightly dilutes the cocktail, and also froths it up deliciously.

4  Strain into punch cups or port glasses, then garnish with a pinch of freshly grated nutmeg and a small slice of orange peel. Cheers!

# SPICED PEAR MARTINI

Deliciously fruity, this cocktail is very dangerous at a party because it almost doesn't taste alcoholic.

YOU WILL NEED
- 50 ml pear vodka
- 15 ml maple or agave syrup
- 10 ml ginger liqueur
- 20 ml lemon juice
- Ground cloves
- Sliced pear and chopped crystallised ginger, to garnish

1  Place all the liquid ingredients in a cocktail shaker. Add a sprinkle of ground cloves and top up with ice. Now do the Tom Cruise bit and shake it all around.

2  Strain the cocktail into well-chilled martini glasses and garnish with a slice of pear and a sprinkling of crystallised ginger.

# CHILDREN'S CHRISTMAS CRAFTS

———

*FUN AND GAMES DURING
THE FESTIVE BUILD-UP*

As December draws near, I'm always tempted to wear a badge that says 'I believe'. Anyone out there harbouring 'non-believers' is advised to sit them down in front of the 1994 remake of *Miracle on 34th Street*. This is a movie I watch time and again with my own boys. The other proof is on the Norad Tracks website (www. noradsanta.org) run by the North American Aerospace Defense Command, which explains the incredible science behind Father Christmas's epic journey around the world on Christmas Eve, and how he makes it to every child's house. We watch him like hawks in ours, knowing that we need to be in bed by the time he gets to Minsk! We leave out ginger biscuits and a tot of whisky for him, and carrots for the reindeer. Since finding the carrot tops scattered over the grass outside the house on Christmas morning two years ago, we now remove the tops because the boys surmised that the reindeer had obviously spat out the bits they didn't like. We couldn't believe it – how rude! Those flying reindeer must think they're a cut above the rest. To be fair, they had come all the way from Fiji, so by the time they arrived at our house, I expect they were pretty tired and emotional.

I find the 'Father Christmas won't come if you're naughty' routine doesn't completely work with my kids, although we did go to Lapland UK last year, and

Father Christmas did a brilliant job of turning my youngest son against the evils of uttering rude words. Remember, nothing is hidden from Father Christmas. He knows everything.

Going that extra mile for the believers is terribly important. I know my kids will let go eventually, but so long as they continue to believe, I fully intend to maintain their illusions. Even our older boys are encouraged to embrace the Father Christmas myth for the sake of the little ones.

There are masses of Christmas crafts for children; I could do a whole book on those alone. Getting children to make things through December is a brilliant way to keep them entertained. I struggle to be glitter-free most of the year, but not a day goes by in December when someone isn't flicking glitter off a coat, out of my hair or off my face. There's a brilliant little craft for glitter baubles on page 212. I made these with a class at my son's school last year, and the year before we made the snow globes on page 204. Although they're included as a children's project, I received an astounding number of tweets from friends and people whose other halves had made snow globes after they saw them on TV.

At school it's a real make fest: the boys come home with cards, wrapping paper, decorations, hats all sorts, and I'm always given presents they've made at Christmas. The local pottery painting café is a firm favourite of theirs, and I have had both birthday and Christmas gifts from there. Two of the Christmas plates are hanging in my bathroom, and the jug and cat I received for my birthday are on my desk. Homemade presents for the teachers go down a treat too.

# TEN LOVELY EXTRAS

Selecting what to put in this chapter was really tough. For every project included I had to reject another twenty, but some are too good to lose entirely, so here are some ideas that I love and that you and the believers in your life can follow up online.

1  Saltdough shapes and letters

2  Paper plate angels

3  Gingerbread biscuits for Father Christmas

4  Egg box bells (I made these with a local school)

5  Paper chains

6  Good old potato-print wrapping paper and cards

7  Christingles

8  Collage

9  Christmas tree angel or star

10  Paper wreath

# NATIVITY SCENE

Making a Nativity scene, with a cradle in a manger, especially one as charming as this, can be a real family event. We have a homemade version in our house and it's lovely to see the children bring it out year after year.

Ms Drake and the amazing children of Redhills Community Primary School in Devon are responsible for this wonderful project. The figures are made with upturned paper cups or that old craft favourite, empty toilet rolls, with a ball for the head. As you can see, all the characters are easily recognisable. The fun is in the embellishments, which can be as simple or as complex as you like. There's no such thing as too much glitter, so you can go to town, especially on the kings. Thank you to Ms Drake and everyone at Redhills Community Primary School. You're a brilliantly artistic bunch.

## *YOU WILL NEED*

———

7 or more ping-pong balls or 50 mm polystyrene balls or homemade balls (see step 2) • Pink paint, for faces and hands • Paintbrushes • Flesh-coloured tights (optional) plus fabric scraps or cotton wool for stuffing • Pink and black pens • PVA glue or glue gun • Wool, for hair and beards • Tracing paper and pencil • Card for arms, crowns and wings, in white, silver and gold • Scissors • Coloured paint, for bodies • At least 7 paper cups or empty toilet rolls (1 each for Mary, Joseph, the three kings, the angel Gabriel, plus as many shepherds as you want) • Scraps of fabric, for clothes (including optional blue, white and striped) • Scraps of ribbon, wool, elastic, pipe cleaners, string or twine, for fastening • Decorations, such as foil, lace, paper doilies, glitter, fur fabric, satin, beads, sequins • Cork or a similar-sized piece of sponge or rolled-up paper or fabric • Empty matchbox, for the manger • Straw or shredded paper • Cardboard box or empty cereal packet, for the stable • Christmas paper (optional) • Twigs (optional)

**HEADS**

1 If using ping-pong balls or polystyrene balls, paint them pink.

2 If you prefer to make your own balls, simply stuff the toe of an old pair of flesh-coloured tights with scrunched-up paper, fabric scraps or cotton wool. Twist the tights until the ball is tight, then tie a knot. To make more heads from the legs of the tights, tie a knot first, then stuff, twist and knot the tights as before.

3 When the heads are ready, use the pink pens to draw rosy cheeks, and the black pen to draw eyes. A nice touch is to draw Mary's eyes like two little smiles as she watches over baby Jesus. The

school used adhesive 'boggly' eyes for particularly friendly characters.

4  For Mary and the angel, glue scraps of wool to the head for hair. For the male figures, glue short pieces of wool to the chin as beards.

### BODIES

5  Trace the arm template on page 235, then transfer it to card as many times as necessary to make two arms per figure. Cut out the shapes and paint the hands pink. Paint the rest of the arms in the colour you want each character to be dressed in, and paint the cup or toilet roll in the same colour. Traditionally, Mary is in blue, the angel in white, and the kings in regal reds, purples and greens, but you can use any colours you like. Set aside to dry.

6  Once the paint is dry, glue the arms to the body and glue the head on top. Allow to dry.

### DRESSING THE FIGURES

7  **For Mary**, make a veil by glueing a square of blue fabric to her head and hold it in place by wrapping a piece of ribbon, wool, elastic or pipe cleaner around it. You can also glue fabric to the body like a shawl if you want more shape, especially if you have used an empty toilet roll.

8  **For Joseph and the shepherds**, make a shawl and a head covering using striped material or natural colours. Experiment with different fabrics, and try using twine or thick string to tie the covering around the head. For the shepherds, shape a pipe cleaner into a crook and glue it behind the hand.

9  **For the angel**, make a halo by twisting a pipe cleaner into shape and taping or glueing it to the back of the head. Trace the wings template on page 235, then transfer it to white, gold or silver card and cut around it. Decorate with foil, lace, borders of paper doilies or glitter and glue them to the angel's back.

10  **For the three kings**, trace the crown template on page 235. Transfer to gold and silver card, then cut out and glue to the relevant heads.

You can be as extravagant as you like when decorating the crowns, using fur fabric, satin, beads, sequins and glitter. Each king should have a cloak and a gift.

11  **For Jesus**, paint the cork pink. When dry, wrap it in a small piece of white fabric, keeping an area clear for the face. Tie the fabric in place with string or ribbon, then draw eyes, nose and a mouth on the face.

### MANGER

12  You can use any small container to make a manger. A matchbox stuffed with straw or shredded paper works well. Alternatively, cut an empty toilet roll in half lengthways, then across the middle and stuff that.

### STABLE

13  Stand a small box or empty cereal packet on its side. Cut along the two short sides and across the top, creating a flap, which is hinged along the bottom edge. Fold the flap down and paint or decorate the box as much as you like. You could simply cover it with Christmas paper, or you could draw cows and donkeys on it, cover the floor with straw or shredded paper, and even stick twigs or straw on the roof. Your characters should be able to display in the open box, and then be stored away in it for next year.

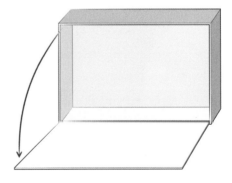

# CHOCOLATE CRISPIE CHRISTMAS TREE

My boys love making chocolate crispie cakes. My youngest had his whole head in the bowl the other day and his hair was covered in the remaining mixture. I have no doubt in my mind that this tree will be adored by children all over the country.

It was with master chocolatier Marc Demarquette that I made my first-ever chocolate crispie Christmas tree. My family and I love them so much I'm sure I'll be making them forever more.

This recipe makes one tree 18 cm high and, apart from the ingredients, you will need at least seven different-sized star cutters, ranging from about 15 cm to 4 cm, or cardboard templates that you can cut around with a small, sharp knife.

## *YOU WILL NEED*

---

375 g milk chocolate · 75 g butter · 6 tbsp golden syrup · 6 tbsp double cream · 3 tbsp cocoa powder · 180 g rice crispies · Decorations, such as sugar balls (mixed with chocolate balls for an all-chocolate tree), sugar stars, edible glitter, icing sugar

### FOR THE BUTTER ICING
100 g softened butter · 200 g icing sugar · 50g cocoa powder, for an all-chocolate tree (optional) · 2–3 tbsp milk · Food colouring (optional)

---

1 Start by making the butter icing. Put the butter into a large mixing bowl and beat until smooth. Add the icing sugar and cocoa powder (if using) and gradually mix together. Once incorporated, beat until smooth. Add enough milk to make an icing that is soft enough to pipe but still firm enough to hold its shape. Add your choice of food colouring (if using). Spoon the butter icing into a piping bag fitted with a small–medium star nozzle and set aside.

2 To make the crispies, put the chocolate, butter, syrup, cream and cocoa powder into a large saucepan. Heat gently until almost melted – you don't want the chocolate to burn. Set aside for about 5 minutes so the last of the chocolate can melt in the residual heat, then mix together so you have a thick, glossy mixture. Add the rice crispies and mix thoroughly.

3 Immediately spread the mixture into a 35 × 25 cm parchment-lined baking tray, smoothing

it into an even layer about 1–1.5 cm thick. Place in the fridge for 30 minutes, or until firm enough to cut (it's easier to cut before fully set).

4 Using your largest cutter, stamp out two stars as close together as possible so you can get maximum stars from the mix. Repeat using the next four sizes of cutter.

5 Now stamp out three stars using the two smallest cutters. In total you should have 16 stars. The offcuts can be cut into small stars to decorate the cake board, or cut into squares and wrapped as 'presents' to go under the tree, or eaten on the spot.

6 Take the largest of the stars and place it in the middle of a serving plate or cake board. Pipe a small dab of butter icing in the middle of the star to act as glue, and top with the other large star, offsetting the points so they aren't directly on top of each other.

7 Repeat with all the remaining stars, stacking them up in descending order of size. If you like, the final small star can stand upright on top of the tree, secured with a swirl of butter icing.

8 Pipe small swirls of butter icing on the tip of each point of the larger stars. As you get higher up the tree you may not have room to pipe on each point, so just pipe every now and then.

9 Take some sugar balls and sugar stars and push them gently into the butter icing swirls. Finish by sprinkling generously with edible glitter. You can also sift over a little icing sugar to look like snow if you like.

10 Store the tree in an airtight container in a cool place. It's best eaten within 2–3 days.

---

*To make an extra large crispie tree you can buy sets of ten star-shaped cutters that range from 20 cm to 5 cm. In this case, you'll need to make half as much crispie mix again.*

---

# MARZIPAN PENGUINS

These marzipan penguins by food stylist Louisa Carter went down a storm at the children's Christmas party Phil and I put on a couple of years ago. If time and energy are on your side, you can make your own marzipan (see page 177); if not, buy the pre-made stuff from the supermarket. There's a fair bit of rolling and food colouring involved, so get the kids to put aprons on before they get stuck in.

## *YOU WILL NEED*

Marzipan · Food colouring in black and orange · Small paintbrush

1  Take a chunk of the marzipan large enough for one penguin (you can make them any size you like) and gently knead to soften it up. Cut off a chunk and roll into a ball to make the body.

2  Next, take two smaller pieces of marzipan and roll into two small balls for the eyes.

3  Take another chunk (enough for the head, wings and feet) and add a few drops of black food colouring. Knead until the colouring is evenly spread through the marzipan, then roll out a ball for the head and two smaller balls for the feet. Attach these to the body by pressing them into place.

4  Now make two oval discs for the wings, making one end wider than the other. Attach the wider end to the side of the body, just below the head. Flick up the narrow end.

5  Attach the eyes to the head, then dip the paintbrush in the black colouring and put a small dot in the middle of each eye.

6  Take the last piece of marzipan and roll into a small cone for the beak. Press this onto the face. Clean your paintbrush with water and paint the beak orange.

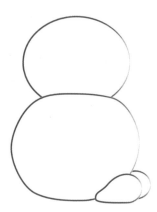

# SNOW GLOBES

Snow globes bring out the child in me. The idea for these little glass balls of joy is thought to have come from 19th-century French paperweights. I've always been mesmerised by the little festive scenes created inside each glass globe, and the way the glitter falls so gently after you shake them. Children always love them – even more so when they've made them themselves.

I enjoyed making them on the show so much that I went into my son's school and taught his whole class how to do it. It was enchanting to see a group of six-year-olds all lined up, totally enthralled with their jars, glitter, water and little figurines ready to stick inside the jar lids. This craft is definitely best done somewhere you don't mind getting a bit messy, so not on the carpet of your neat and tidy sitting room. Then again, that's true for all little person crafts. You will need a glue gun, which you'll have to be the master of in front of the children as it becomes extremely hot.

Trust me, snow globes go down a storm with the kids.

## *YOU WILL NEED*

---

Glass jars with lids (screw-top honey jars and baby food jars work well) • Enamel paint • Paintbrush • Hairdryer (optional) • Plastic or ceramic figurines (such as Santa and snowmen), plus mini Christmas trees • Glue gun or tube of strong glue • 1 litre filtered water • Glitter (white works well) • Glycerine (available from pharmacies)

1  Start by painting the jar lids. This is optional, but I do it to cover any brand names and make them really Christmassy in colour. They'll need two coats and must be left to dry between each one. You can speed up the drying process with a hairdryer if anyone is getting impatient.

2  Turn the dried lids painted side down and get the children to arrange their figurines inside the lids. When happy with the arrangement, take the figures out, apply a generous coat of glue inside the lid and stick the arrangement back in place. Set aside until completely dry.

3  Fill the jar almost to the top with filtered water. Add a teaspoon of glitter and a dash of glycerine. The glycerine is the magic stuff that thickens the water and creates a snowfall effect with the glitter.

4  There are two options for sealing the jars: you can either glue them shut so they are forever safe from inquisitive fingers, or you can just screw the lid on very tightly.

*Painting the lids could be done before the children get stuck in, which will avoid them having to wait for lengthy drying times.*

*Add a festive gift tag to the neck of the jar for additional decoration, or to give it as a present.*

*If your figures come loose from vigorous shaking, just empty out the jars and dry thoroughly. Reglue everything in place and fill them with filtered water, glitter and glycerine again.*

# PAPER CORNUCOPIAS

Whilst filming *Kirstie's Vintage Christmas*, I went to Munich to visit the city's extraordinary Christmas market. German Christmas markets are the real deal, with rows and rows of little wooden stalls, fairy lights, and the delicious aroma of mulled wine in the cold air.

During my visit, I made these mini Christmas cornucopias to hang on the Christmas tree. They are a brilliant craft for little ones, especially when you've got a million things to do and you just want to occupy the kids with something quiet and not particularly messy. The cornucopias can be filled with sweets and treats, then hung on the tree as Christmas favours for their friends or guests. All you need is some strong paper and decorative bits and pieces you probably have lying around the house.

## *YOU WILL NEED*

---

Small round cereal bowl • Strong wrapping paper or old wallpaper • Pencil • Scissors • Glue • Decorations, such as festive stickers or cut-outs, beads, sequins, glitter, etc. • Narrow ribbon • Butterfly clips • Sweets and small treats

1 Place the bowl upside down on the paper, draw around it and then cut out the circle.

2 Fold the circle in half, make a sharp crease and tear or cut along it. The two halves will create two cornucopias.

3 Fold the straight side of each semicircle in half to create a cone shape. Glue along one side, overlap the other side and stick them together. Allow to dry.

4 Decorate the cone by glueing on little festive stickers (stars, holly leaves, etc.), or cut-outs from old Christmas cards, beads, buttons or sequins and glitter .

5 Cut a length of narrow ribbon to act as a handle and attach it to either side of the cornucopia's opening with butterfly clips, or make two holes, one on each side, with a hole punch and thread the ribbon through, securing it with a knot. Fill the cornucopias with sweets or little treats and hang them from the Christmas tree.

---

*To minimise fraying, always cut the ends of ribbon at an angle.*

---

# PARTY JELLY

Jelly on a plate, jelly on a plate, wibble wobble, wibble wobble, jelly on a plate. That's the rhyme you have to sing whilst giving this sweet party jelly a try. It was Sam Bompas of Bompas & Parr, jelly-makers supreme, who showed me how to create this fresh fruit jelly masterpiece using sandcastle buckets as moulds. It's easy and really delicious, but if you don't have time to go through the fruit straining, I've invented a little short cut of my own. Sam, read no further . . . I use two packets of orange jelly dissolved in just enough water, and then top it up with fresh blood orange juice for flavour and good colour.

Sam's method is perfect for a fun dinner party dessert where you'll want to do things properly. My short cut isn't bad either for a really busy grown-up with kids chomping at the bit for a bucketful of sweetie jelly.

## YOU WILL NEED

1 kg plums (or virtually any fruit you have to hand) · About 120 g sugar · Muslin cloth and sieve · Juice of ½ lemon · 5 sheets gelatine (platinum grade is the highest quality, and available from most supermarkets) · Small sweets or chunks of fresh fruit (optional)

1  Put the plums in a saucepan with a small amount of water and sprinkle with 20 g of the sugar. Cover and simmer on the hob until the fruit is soft and mushy.

2  Put a muslin cloth over a sieve and place over a measuring jug. Pour the mushy plums into the cloth and leave to drip until you have 300 ml plum juice in the jug. This can take a while, so be patient. Don't force the juice through or it will become cloudy.

3  In a saucepan, dissolve the remaining sugar in 100 ml water to make a thin syrup. Pour into the plum juice, add another 100 ml water and the lemon juice and mix together in the jug.

4  Put the gelatine and a little of the plum liquid into a heatproof bowl and set over a saucepan of boiling water (the bowl should not touch the water). Heat, stirring constantly, until the gelatine has dissolved – about 2 minutes.

5  Sieve the gelatine mixture into the jug of juice and stir thoroughly.

6  Pour half the mixture into a 500 ml mould. Alternatively, for single servings use 50ml moulds. If you want to add sweets or chunks of fresh fruit, put them in at this stage, then top up the mould with the rest of the mixture. Place in the fridge for 6 hours.

7  To turn out, dip the mould in hot water for 10 seconds to release the jelly, then invert onto a plate to serve.

# TEA-LIGHT LANTERNS

The children from Redhills Primary School in Exeter made these lovely tea-light lanterns with their teacher, Ms Drake, as a gift for me after we came second in a scarecrow-making competition at a local country show – which we should have won...

This is an activity that all ages can get stuck into and be as creative as their heart desires. The result is a real thrill, admired without fail by everyone who sees it. The tissue paper makes the lanterns super-colourful, and if you and your clan make plenty, you can put them all around the house – on hooks, along windowsills, above fireplaces, even lighting up the garden path.

Candles are a great way to bring a little bit of light and fun into the darkest winter days, and with this little craft it's a real joy.

## *YOU WILL NEED*

———

Clean jam jar, big enough to hold a tea-light candle · Coloured tissue paper or Decoupatch paper in Christmas colours · Pencil · Scissors · Paintbrush · PVA glue · Glitter · Florist's wire, for a handle · Small pliers · Christmas charms, beads or decorations · Tea-light candles

1 Start by decorating your jar. Draw small shapes, such as squares, stars and Christmas trees, on the tissue paper and cut them out.

2 Paint some PVA glue onto the jar where you want to place your first tissue shape. Apply the paper and smooth it from the centre to the edges. Wipe away any excess glue. Overlap the first paper shape with a second so they meet seamlessly. Apply glue and smooth out as before. Continue until the jar is covered with your chosen design. For a sparkly effect, stick glitter around the outside.

3 To make a handle, bend a length of wire around the neck of the jar. Make a small loop at one end of it and thread the other end through. Form a hook in the loose end of the wire, bend it over the jar opening and tuck it under the neck

wire on the opposite side. For a pretty effect, thread charms, beads or Christmas decorations onto the wire before it's secured.

4 Pop a candle into the jar, light it and enjoy.

Putting a generous handful of sand in the bottom of the jar will prevent the tea-light from sliding around.

The tissue paper shapes can be stamped rather than drawn if you have shape stampers. These are great for little kids.

# GLITTER BAUBLES

I made these baubles with a class of schoolchildren, and they went down very well. They were great fun to create and look lovely in lots of different colours, shapes and sizes. Applying PVA glue is a bit like make-up: the trick is to use a thin layer – just enough to keep the bits and pieces stuck, but not so much that it slips off when left to dry.

Obviously, you'll be picking glitter off your face for weeks after this one.

## YOU WILL NEED

Polystyrene balls · Cocktail sticks or wooden skewers · Paintbrush · PVA glue · Fine glitter · Plastic tub or baking tray · Old shoebox · Ribbon · Paper clips or thin wire

1 Impale a polystyrene ball on a stick so you can hold it like a lollipop. Paint the ball with a thin layer of PVA glue, making sure it's well covered. Don't dip it in the glue or it will drip when drying and ruin the bauble.

2 Put the fine glitter into an old ice cream tub or baking tray and roll the ball, still on the stick, around in the glitter until completely covered. Use a teaspoon to sprinkle glitter onto any hard-to-reach areas.

3 Turn the shoebox upside down, push the bauble stick through the bottom of it and leave the bauble to dry overnight.

4 Decide where your bauble is going to hang, then cut a double length of ribbon. With a pin or thin piece of wire bent into a U-shape, pierce the centre of the ribbon and push it into the bauble. Knot the ribbon ends together and hang the bauble on the tree.

*To create a stripy ball, apply lines of glue and sprinkle different colours of glitter onto each one.*

# CHRISTMAS COOKIES

I once had the privilege of making cookies for Father Christmas in Lapland. I'll do anything to get into his good books. If you want to try bribing him, I highly recommend this recipe by the super food stylist Louisa Carter. Get the kids to make the cookies with you, and cut them into festive shapes, such as stars, Christmas trees, penguins, reindeer, snowmen and angels. The basic icing can be divided into several batches, each coloured differently, and of course you can decorate with sugar sprinkles, silver balls and edible glitter for extra Christmas sparkle.

This recipe makes about 20, depending on size and shape.

## *YOU WILL NEED*

200 g softened butter · 200 g sugar · 1 large egg, lightly beaten · ½ tsp vanilla extract or 1 tsp ground mixed spice (optional) · 375 g plain flour, plus extra for dusting · 1–2 tbsp milk, if needed · Decorations, such as sugar sprinkles, silver balls, desiccated coconut (for snow) and edible glitter

### FOR THE ICING
1 large egg white · 300 g icing sugar · Juice of ½ lemon · Various food colourings

1  To make the cookies, cream the butter and sugar together until light and fluffy. Add the egg and vanilla or spice and beat the mixture until well combined. Add the flour and mix to form a soft dough, pouring in a splash of milk to help it bind if necessary.

2  Shape the dough into a thick circle roughly 20 cm in diameter, wrap in cling film and rest in the fridge for about 15 minutes.

3  Preheat the oven to 160°C/Gas 3. Line 3–4 baking sheets with parchment.

4  On a very lightly floured work surface, roll out the dough to a thickness of 4–5 mm. You might find it easier to do this in two batches.

5  Using whatever size and type of cutters you like, stamp out various shapes. Transfer them to the prepared trays with a palette knife, spacing them about 2 cm apart so they have room to expand. Reroll any offcuts and repeat until all the dough has been used.

6  Bake the cookies for 10–12 minutes, or until golden brown at the edges. Transfer them to wire racks to cool.

7  To make the icing, lightly beat the egg white into soft peaks. Gradually add the icing sugar, beating each addition, until the mixture is stiff and glossy. Add the lemon juice and, if necessary, a splash of water if the icing is too stiff. If not using the icing straight away, cover it with cling film to stop it from drying out.

8  Spoon some of the white icing into a piping bag fitted with a small, plain nozzle and pipe outlines around each cookie, just a few millimetres in from the edge; this will help to contain the coloured icing that you are going to fill it with. For more elaborate designs, such as an angel or a reindeer, also pipe lines for the wings, the dress and the antlers.

9  Divide the remaining icing between separate bowls, depending how many colours you want, and mix a few drops of food colouring into each bowl. Add a little cold water to thin the icing slightly, then spoon it inside the piped outlines prepared in step 8. Scatter with sugar sprinkles or sugar shapes and leave to set.

10  Once the icing has set, you can pipe more details on top if you like, using the thicker icing.

*If you want an easier method of decoration for young children, or if you don't want to use raw egg, make a basic icing using just icing sugar and water, mixed to the consistency of double cream (too thin and it will run off; too thick and it won't stick very easily, so it's best to start thick and add more water a drop at a time). Divide the icing and mix in different colours (as in step 9), then dip just the top of the cookies in it to coat. Place on a wire rack so any excess icing can drip off, and sprinkle with edible glitter, sparkles, Smarties, Jelly Tots or sugar shapes.*

*Names and other words can be piped in thick sugar and water icing, or you can buy ready-made 'writing icing' to add details once the basic icing has set.*

# DIRECTORY

---

**Fran Baigent**
*Embroiderer*
franbaigent@aol.com

**Alice Begg**
*Designer*
humphriesandbegg.co.uk
info@humphriesandbegg.co.uk

**Sam Bompas**
*Jelly Expert*
bompasandparr.co.uk
020 7403 9403

**Kate Brett**
*Paper Marbling*
payhembury.com
kate@payhembury.com

**Louisa Carter**
*Home Economist and Food Writer*
louisacarter.com
louisa@louisacarter.com

**Poppy Chancellor**
*Illustrator and Paper-cut Artist*
poppychancellor.com
poppychancellor@me.com

**Linda Clift**
*Antique Textiles*
antiquequiltsandtextiles.co.uk
01305 264914

**The Cloth Shop**
theclothshop.net
theclothshop@gmail.com

**Jo Colwill**
*Quilter*
cowslipworkshops.co.uk
info@cowslipworkshops.co.uk

**David Constable**
*Candle-maker*
candlemakers.co.uk
mail@candlemakers.co.uk

**Karyl Cragg**
*Textile Designer*
drawntothevalley.co.uk
sarah@dttv.co.uk

**Victoria Cranfield**
*Maker of Jam, Marmalade, Chutney,*
*Condiments and Jelly*
cranfieldsfoods.co.uk
info@cranfieldsfoods.com

**Curwen Studio**
*High-quality Fine Art Prints*
thecurwenstudio.co.uk
info@thecurwenstudio.co.uk

**Rosie Davies**
*Cookery teacher*
rosiedavies.co.uk
01373 836210

**Christa Davis**
*Clothes Designer*
christadavis.com
contact@christadavis.com

**Marc Demarquette**
*Chocolatier*
demarquette.com
info@demarquette.com

**Amanda Drake**
*School Administrator and Crafter*
Redhills Primary School
01392 255555

**Jenny Elesmore**
*Soap-maker*
oddsandsuds.com
shop@oddsandsuds.com

**Jayne Emerson**
*Textile Designer*
jayneemerson.co.uk
jayneemerson@hotmail.com

**English Stamp Company**
*Rubber Stamp-makers*
englishstamp.com
01929 439117

**Jonathan Gibb**
*Designer*
centralillustration.com
info@ centralillustration.com

**Farmer Guy**
*Ham-maker*
farmerguy.co.uk
guy@farmerguy.com

**Clare Gould**
*Calligrapher*
english-wedding.com

**Kitten Grayson**
*Florist*
kittenandco.com
hello@kittenandco.com

**Richard Hunt**
*Chef*
grandtorquay.co.uk
info@grandtorquay.co.uk

**Clare Hutchison**
*Cracker-maker*
froufrouandthomas.co.uk
info@froufrouandthomas.co.uk

**James Harvey Furniture**
*Furniture Designer*
jamesharveyfurniture.com
contact@jamesharveyfurniture.com

**Susie Johnson**
*Knitter*
thewoolsanctuary.com
susiejohnson1@btinternet.com

**Judd Street Papers**
*Cracker Paper Supplier*
juddstreetgallery.com2.html

**Georgie Kirby**
*Bunting Designer and Maker*
bigbeautifulbunting.com
info@bigbeautifulbunting.co.uk

**Polly Lyster**
*Dyeing and Textiles*
dyeworks.co.uk
thedyeworks@mac.com

**James MacKenzie**
*Chef*
pipeandglass.co.uk
email@pipeandglass.co.uk

**Susan McCann**
*Food Producer*
simplyaddchilli.com
susan@simplyaddchilli.com

**Joe McCanta**
*Mixologist*
pursip.com
joe@pursip.com

**Jane Means**
*Wrapping Expert*
janemeans.co.uk
info@janemeans.co.uk

**Jaina Minton**
*Designer and Crafter*
polkadotsundays.com
jaina@polkadotsundays.com

**Paperchase**
*Stationery Supplier*
paperchase.co.uk

**Scott Paton**
*Chef*
thehornofplenty.co.uk
enquiries@thehornofplenty.co.uk

**Clare Pentlow**
*Designer and Maker*
cjpdesigns.co.uk
clare.pentlow@hotmail.co.uk

**Susan Read**
*Chocolatier*
bigridgechocolates.co.uk
bigridgechocolates@yahoo.co.uk

**Cat Rowe**
*Textile Designer*
textileillustration.co.uk

**Zeena Shah**
*Textile Designer*
zeenashah.com
hello@zeenashah.com

**Mandy Shaw**
*Textile Designer and Quilter*
dandeliondesigns.co.uk

**Tavistock Embroiderers**
*Embroiderers*
embroiderersguild.com
administrator@embroiderersguild.com

**Andy Thompstone**
*Cider-maker*
thompstonescider.co.uk
andy@thompstonescider.co.uk

**Sue Timney**
*Interior Designer*
suetimney.co.uk
enquiries@suetimney.com

**Isabelle Ting**
*Bookbinder*
owlandlion.com

**Volga Linen**
volgalinen.co.uk
info@volgalinen.co.uk

# *TEMPLATES*

———

All the templates are drawn on a 5 cm grid (one small square equals 1 cm). Most of the templates are drawn actual size, so they can simply be traced and cut out. In each case, cut out any black or grey areas too. You might find this easier to do with a craft knife than a pair of scissors.

A few of the templates, such as the Oversized Christmas Stocking, are reduced to a percentage of their full size. The percentage is noted below the template and can be scaled up to whatever size you like.

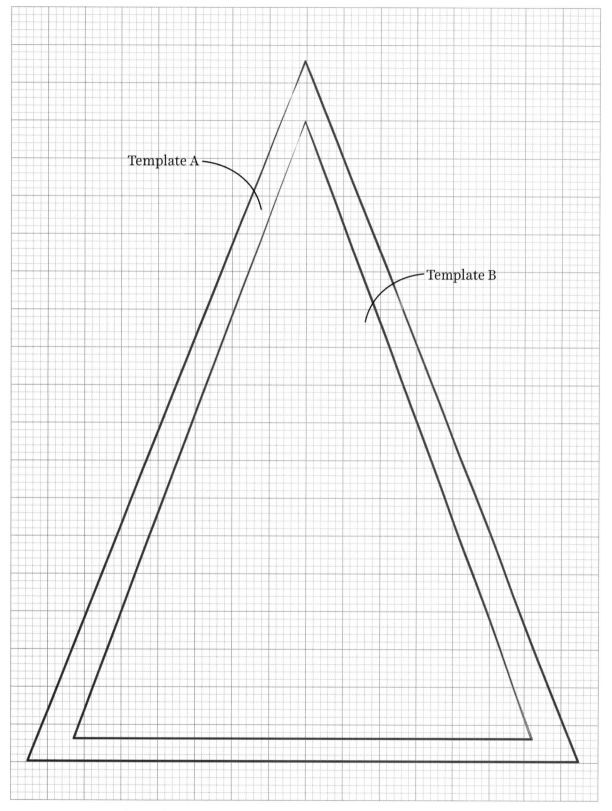

Template A

Template B

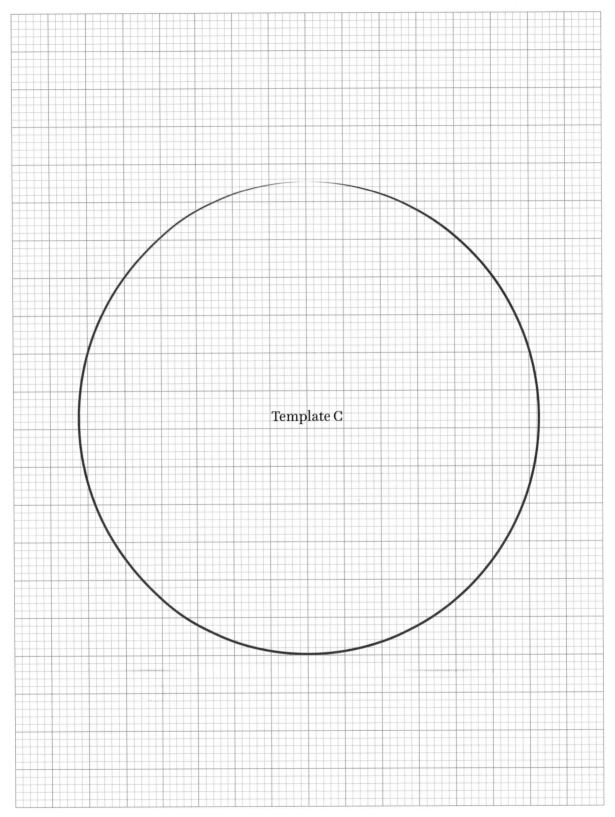

Template C

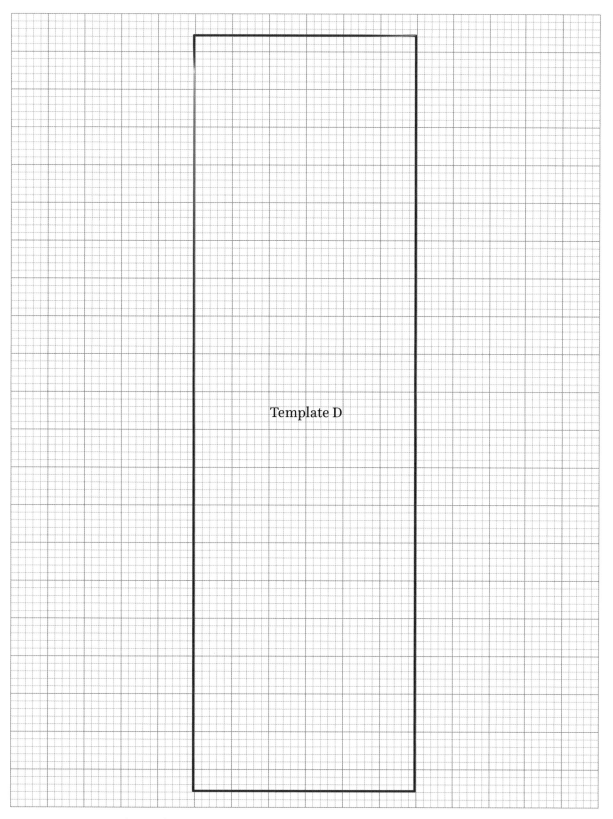

Template D

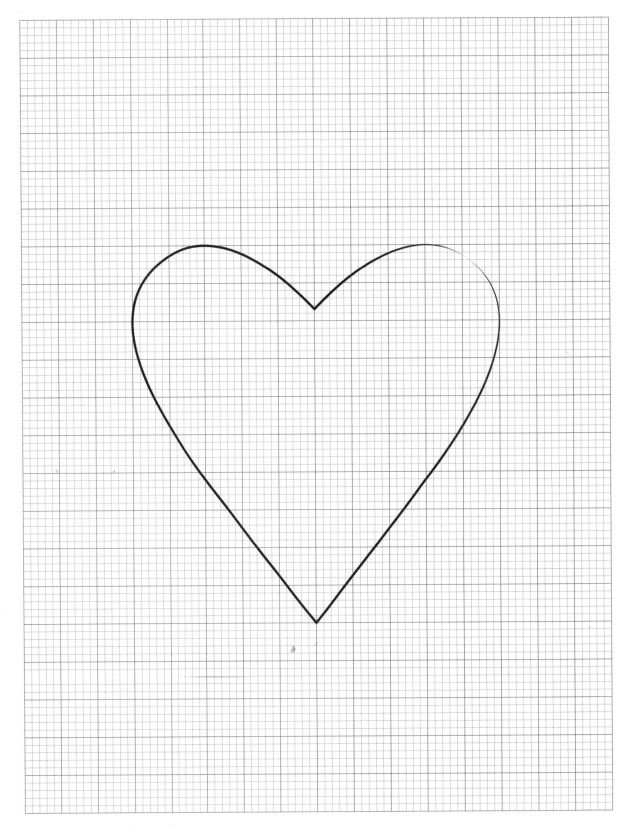

**HEART GARLAND** (page 12)

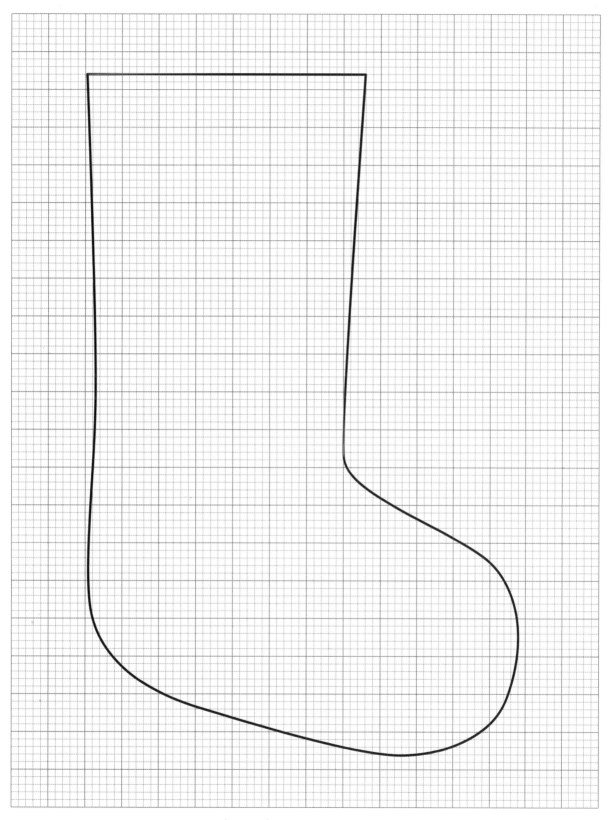

OVERSIZED CHRISTMAS STOCKING (page 20)                                    25%

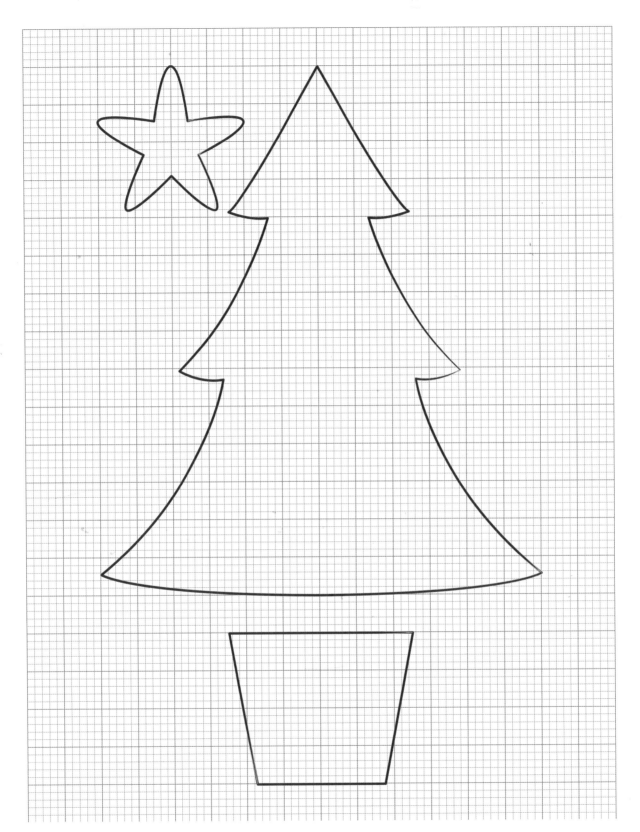

**QUILTED ADVENT CALENDAR** (page 37)

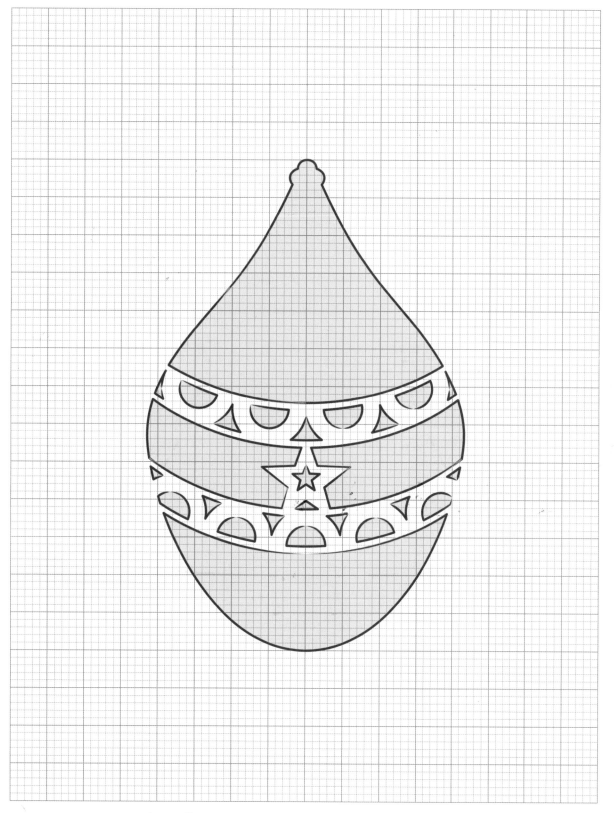

**FABRIC WINDOW CARD** (page 56)

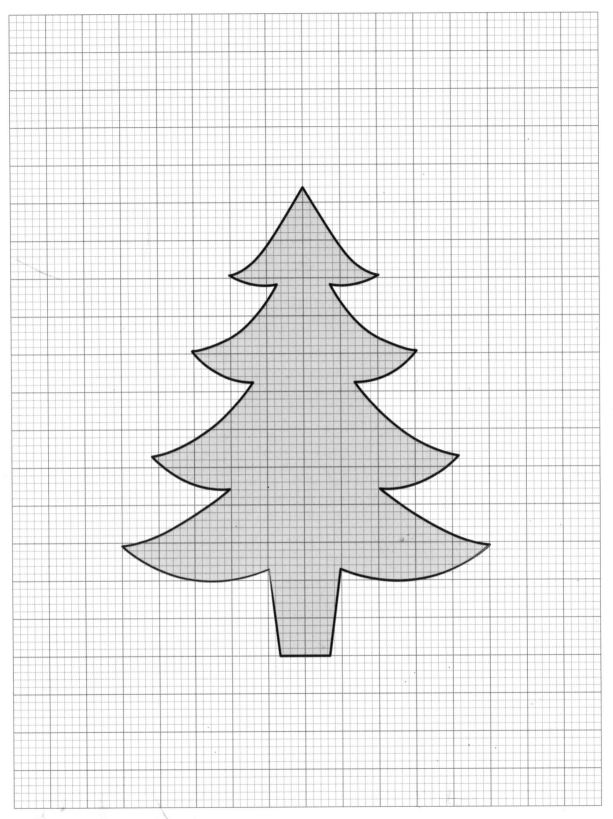

FABRIC WINDOW CARD (page 56)

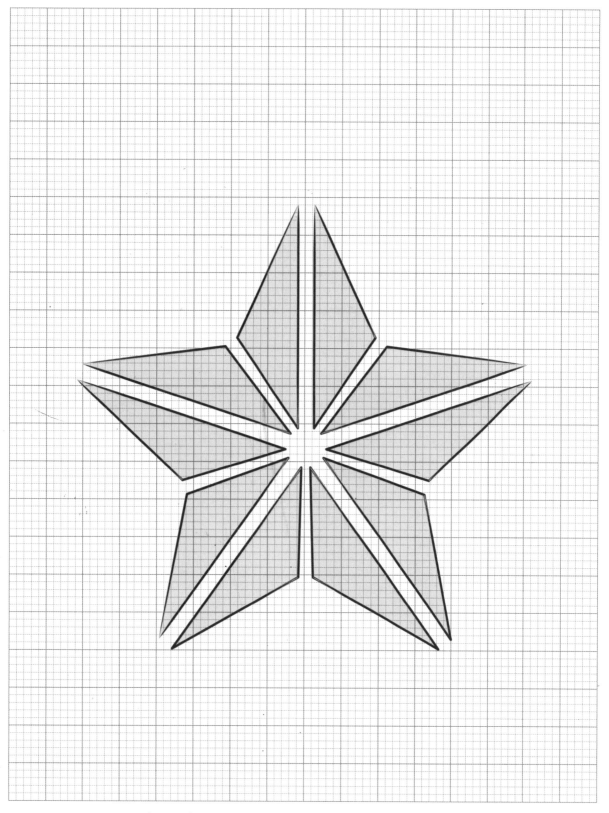

FABRIC WINDOW CARD (page 56)

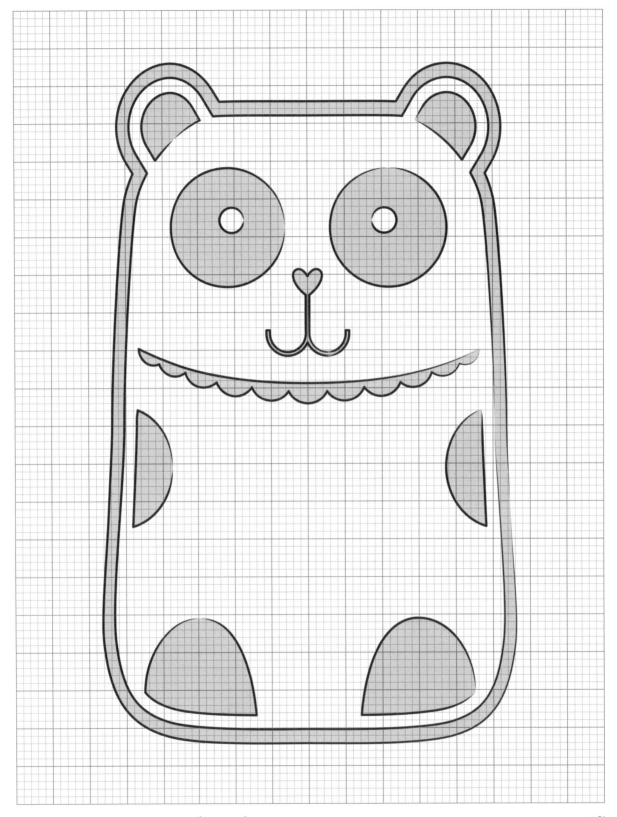

**SCREEN-PRINTED TOY PANDA** (page 114)                                  75%

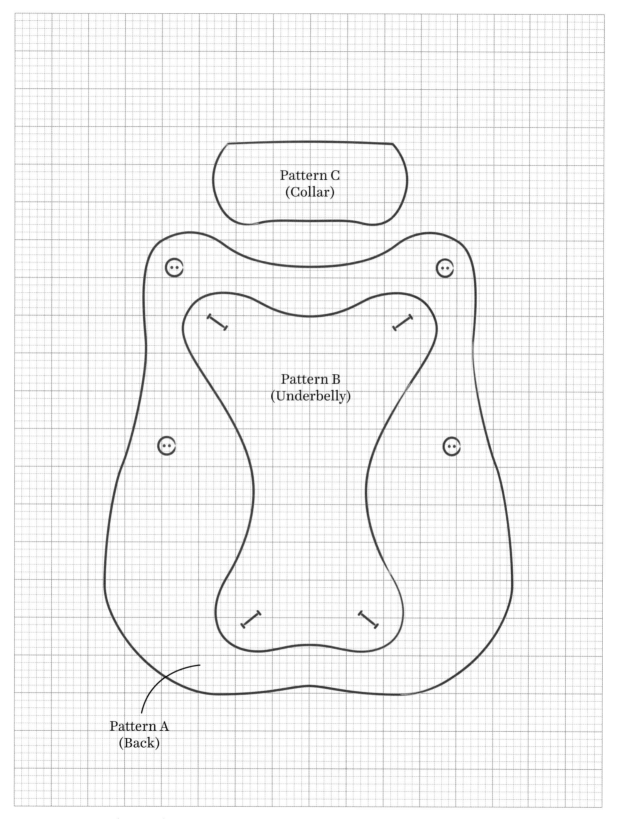

Pattern C
(Collar)

Pattern B
(Underbelly)

Pattern A
(Back)

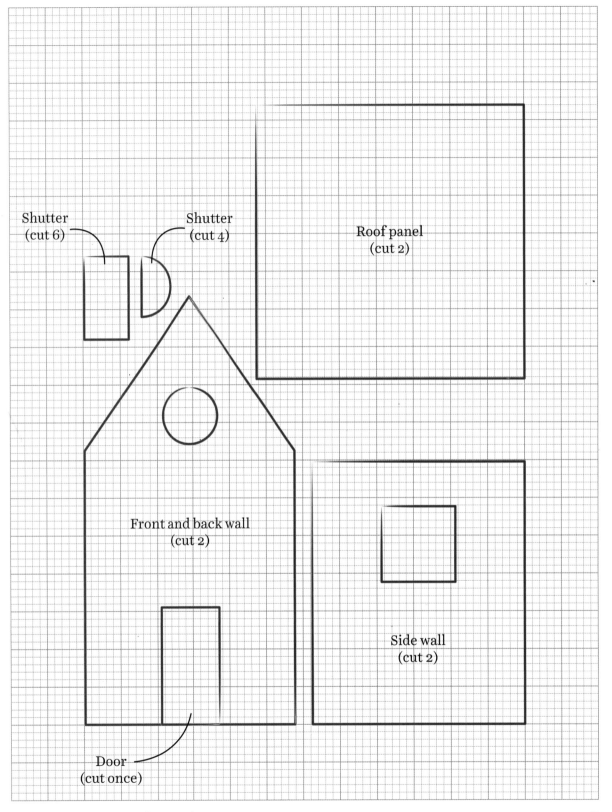

Shutter
(cut 6)

Shutter
(cut 4)

Roof panel
(cut 2)

Front and back wall
(cut 2)

Side wall
(cut 2)

Door
(cut once)

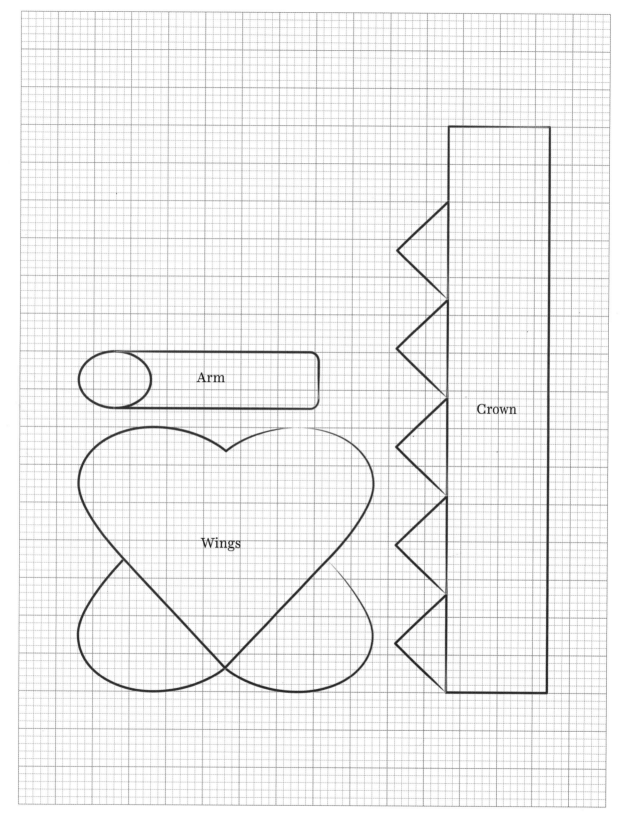

Arm

Crown

Wings

# EMBROIDERY STITCHES

There are loads of embroidery stitches to choose from, ranging from the downright simple to the fiendishly complicated. Here we offer just a small selection that can be used for the various projects in this book. If you want an even wider choice, visit your local library or go online. It's amazing what can be done with a needle and thread.

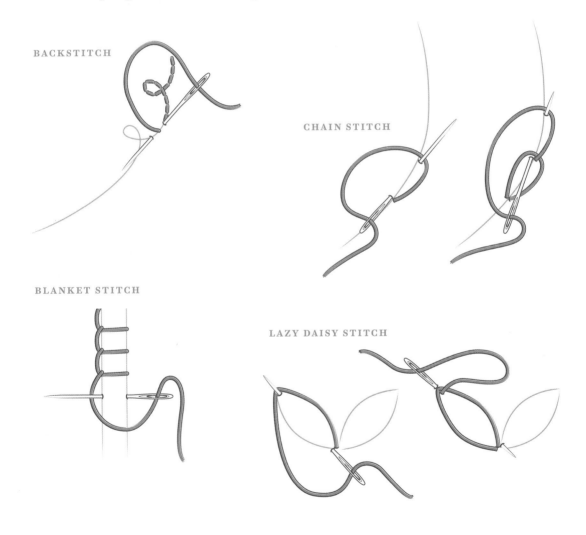

BACKSTITCH

CHAIN STITCH

BLANKET STITCH

LAZY DAISY STITCH

## FISHBONE STITCH

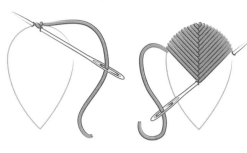

## OPEN FISHBONE STITCH

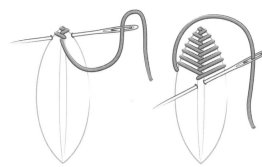

## FLY STITCH

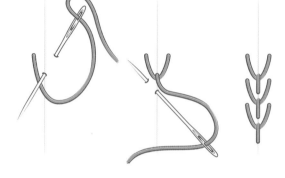

## STEM STITCH

## PEKINESE STITCH

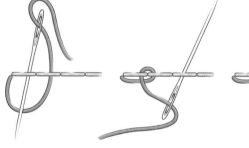

## SATIN STITCH

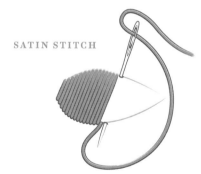

## FRENCH KNOT

## DOUBLE KNOT STITCH

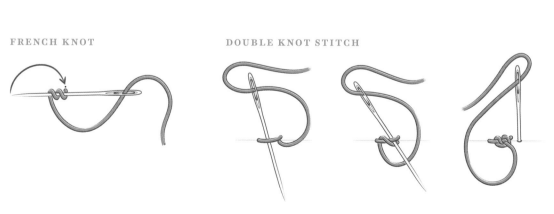

# *INDEX*

# ACKNOWLEDGEMENTS

Christmas wouldn't be Christmas if it weren't for all the amazing people who have been involved in all of the Christmas TV shows over the years. You all know who you are. From the creative skills of the crafts people to the crew and the very talented team at Raise the Roof Productions, this book is for all of you.

Jane Muirhead is the gold star on top of the tree and Sarah Walmsley is the angel looking out for me, whilst Lisa McCann and Jamie Stimpson sprinkle bucketfuls of glitter all over the show making Christmas look beautiful. Andrew Jackson is a cracker, always playing a huge part in the festivities. Jeannot Hutcheson is one of the loveliest people I know; kind, talented and incredibly hard working. Fiona Murray is the saint who has taken so many lovely photographs, working patiently and quietly whilst we were filming.

Also, thank you to the amazing Sasha and Simon Schwerdt who let us in to their beautiful and inspiring home, which set the scene for so many wonderful projects. We had the shoot of our lives and it really shows in the pictures.

I am hugely grateful to everyone at Channel 4 – Kate Teckman, Karoline Copping, Clemency Green, Hanna Warren, Gill Wilson and Jay Hunt who have let us make four years of Christmas craft shows. I never want to stop.

I am also very grateful to Nicky Ross, Sarah Hammond, Trish Burgess, Leni Lawrence, Clare Skeats, Nicky Barneby, Al Oliver and all the team at Hodder, who believed a Christmas book would knock everyone's stockings off.

To Beth, who makes *everything* better, and my agent Hilary at Arlington Enterprises who is a rock. The home team of Natasha, Heather, Maravic, Angelina, Chrissie and Sophie, are such a big part of all of these pages.

Finally, thank you to my family, Ben and the boys, who are the spirit of my Christmas.

## SNOWFLAKE APPEAL

It's so important to stop and think about those families for whom Christmas is a very difficult time. For the last couple of years I've been working hard to raise awareness for Home-Start, a remarkable charity for which I have become an ambassador.

Home-Start helps 70,000 vulnerable children every year via their 16,000 trained volunteers. They have recently launched their Snowflake Appeal to raise vital funds for the amazing work they do with vulnerable children and families at Christmas.

This is a fantastic organisation and whether you volunteer, fundraise, or make a donation, there is no better thing to do for those children who won't have the special Christmas that your children, nephews, nieces or grand-children are lucky enough to have.

For more information about Home-Start and the Snowflake Appeal go to home-start.org.uk, facebook.com/homestartuk or twitter.com/homestartuk.